AF552869

ENERGY AND URBANISATION

ENERGY AND URBANISATION

By

Dr. M. Lakshmi Narasaiah
M.A., Ph.D.
Professor of Economics
Co-ordinator, Dept. of M.B.A. and Commerce
Special Officer
Sri Krishnadevaraya University Post-graduate Centre
Kurnool–518 002
Andhra Pradesh
(India)

DISCOVERY PUBLISHING HOUSE PVT. LTD.
NEW DELHI-110 002

First Published-2008

ISBN 978-81-8356-308-6

Published by:

DISCOVERY PUBLISHING HOUSE PVT. LTD.
4831/24, Ansari Road, Prahlad Street,
Darya Ganj, New Delhi-110002 (India)
Phone: 23279245 • Fax: 91-11-23253475
E-mail: dphbooks@rediffmail.com
dphtemp@indiatimes.com
Website: www.discoverypublishinghouse.com

Printed at
Arora Offset Press
Laxmi Nagar, Delhi–92

Preface

The world's cities are growing far faster than its population. Indeed, aside from the growth of population itself, urbanisation is the dominant demographic trend of the half-century now ending. In 1950, 750 million of the world's people lived in cities. By 1996, this had at least tripled, to more than 2.6 billion. The number projected to live in cities by 2050, some 6.5 billion people, exceeds world population today.

Urbanisation on anything like the scale that we know today is historically quite recent. In 1800, only one city, London, had a million people. Today, 326 cities have at least that many people. And there are 14 mega cities, those with 10 million or more residents. Tokyo is the largest, at 27 million. Mexico city is second, at 17 million. New York city and Sao Paulo are close behind, with 16 million each. Rounding out the list in descending size are Bombay (15 million), Shanghai (14), Los Angeles (12), Calcutta (12), Buenos Aires (12), Beijing (11), Osaka (11), Lagos (10), Rio de Janeiro (10), and Delhi (10).

The rate of growth of cities in industrial countries during the first century or so of the Industrial Revolution was relatively slow. Today's cities are growing much faster. It took London 130 years to get from 1 million to 8 million. Mexico city made this jump in just 30 years.

Dr. M. Lakshmi Narasaiah

Contents

1

Energy and Sustainability

Mankind's history is marked by a growing use of energy which until the end of the Industrial Revolution came largely from renewable sources. It was coal that fed the furnaces and boilers of the Industrial Revolution from the end of the seventeenth century to the nineteenth century, and drove railway transport and steamships. As well as being a useful source of mechanical energy, it was also used in the manufacture of coal gas for street lighting and in the chemical industry. In fact, coal was the principal form of energy until 1900.

Discoveries at the beginning of the nineteenth century allowed the use of electricity and revealed the relations and the interconvertibility of different forms of energy. The principles of conservation and of energy quality did not become operative until much later. Meanwhile, in 1882, the first system for producing and distributing electricity in a large city was installed. This was the beginning of the second phase in industrialisation through electrification.

Following the first successful oil drillings in 1859, Standard Oil, the first of the modern large scale oil companies, attempted the first vertical structure for overall control of the oil process. It involved extraction from the subsoil, storage, refining and final distribution. Later, the growth of derivatives, the lower extraction costs compared to coal and the greater ease and economy of transport made oil modern society's basic energy source.

The internal combustion engine led to motorisation on a massive scale by land, sea and air and guaranteed a constantly growing market for petrol. The forties marked the start of the new petrochemical industry, which gave rise to an enormous number of new products; synthetic rubber, plastic, medicines, cosmetics, varnishes, artificial fibres, detergents, weedkillers, fertilizers, butane, propane, etc., opening the way to the mass-production of consumer goods and introducing new, non-biodegradable substances into the environment.

After World War II, ambitious programmes to produce electricity from nuclear energy were begun, in the search for a return on the enormous amounts of money invested. The economic expansion in the West during the fifties and sixties was directly related to enormous petrol consumption at a time when energy was considered plentiful and cheap. Energy consumption during these decades grew more than exponentially. The fastest developing industrial sectors were precisely the ones that consumed most energy—petrochemical industries, metallurgy, car manufacturing, domestic appliances, electricity generating, etc.—and a trend developed towards goods and services with higher energy intensity. Since 1950, increased energy production has been systematically favoured over more rational use. So much so that the increase in energy consumption has been taken as a reliable indicator of progress.

The Aftermath of the Oil Boom

The oil crises of 1973 and 1980 showed up the fragility of an energy system that was over-dependent on oil. The War in the Gulf was reminder of what was at stake for the Western economies; free access to cheap oil in the Middle East. It was therefore fear of the hardship caused by the first crisis that brought about a change in attitudes in Western countries; efforts were directed at breaking free from this dependence, diversifying supply sources, perfecting replacement energies and promoting energy-saving programmes.

The eighties marked a change in people's awareness about environmental problems. The damage was making itself felt in more and more places and eventually the global threat to our planet as a result of our energy system became clear; the composition of the atmosphere was changing and could lead to possible changes in the climate.

According to recent figures, 82 per cent of all the energy consumed in the world is produced by burning fossil fuels, 7.5 per cent from burning biomass, 5.5 per cent from the use of hydraulic energy and 5 per cent from nuclear energy. Most of our energy in other words, in non-renewable; it runs out as we use it, as the population increases; and it comes from fossil fuels, which on burning increase the amount of CO_2 in the atmosphere. If we add to this the accumulation of nuclear waste, the problems of access to oil deposits, constant spillages during transport and all the different imbalances involved in the world energy system, the outlook is far from sustainable.

The inequalities speak for themselves; globally, less than a quarter of the world's richest population consumes almost three quarters of the energy commercialised in the world. For example, the average annual consumption per capita in the United States is 26 times higher than in India.

The Choice of Change

Opening the way to societies that make sustainable use of energy necessarily involves increasing and improving energy efficiency, both in supply technologies and in end-use technologies, at the same time using renewable energy sources instead of fossil fuels.

Choosing the right system for the transformation of primary energy sources into energy services such as lighting, cooling, cooking, mechanical force, transport, etc. and choosing the most suitable appliances and technologies in each case is fundamental.

The truth is that a good standard of living is possible without wasting anything like as much energy. A series of relatively straightforward measures today allow a far higher level of comfort than in 1950, using one-third as much energy for heating water for washing in the home.

Petrol consumption by vehicles has dropped by 40 per cent in forty years, from 8 litres/100 kilometres to 5.3 litres in some models, and the work of improving their energy efficiency continues. In industry, the energy consumption necessary for manufacturing large intermediary products (steel, cement, paper or fertilizer) is decreasing steadily at a rate which varies between 0.5 per cent and 0.2 per cent per year according to the product.

Today's incandescent bulbs consume one twentieth as much electricity as bulbs in the twenties. The compact fluorescent bulbs now available can cut this down again to one-fifth. Efficiency in lighting has increased one-hundredfold. The use of new materials and a more rational use of traditional materials allows a reduction in the amount of energy and raw materials consumed. Building a house, for example, requires 20 per cent less energy than in 1950; building a vehicle, 40 per cent less. On a global level, reducing our society's energy-intensiveness is the first step towards energy sustainability.

❄ ❄ ❄

2

Energy
A Fair Deal for All

Both the supply of energy and the demand for it have spiralled in modern societies, where everyday life and changes to the environment, global as well as local, are conditioned by energy production and use. There is a crying need for a fairer share-out of material goods, energy and economic resources.

Energy comes in three forms: So-called "fossil" fuels (coal, oil and natural gas); nuclear power; and "renewable" energies (hydroelectric power, thermal or photovoltaic solar energy, wind and tide power, wood, etc.). Each of these has its own undeniable advantages and drawbacks.

Fossil Fuels

Fossil fuels are abundant and very simple to use. Oil, for example, can be very easily transported and processed, and is relatively cheap. The technology for producing its many derivatives is highly developed. What's more, it is particularly well suited for use in all forms of land, sea and air transport. Its handy fluid form and its price make it appropriate to the needs of poor communities or those that are unable to invest in capital goods.

Fossil fuels account at present for 77 per cent of all the energy produced and will, according to the most realistic projections, still account for 73 per cent in 2020. The resources will be strictly limited geographically as well as in duration, being restricted to certain regions. This state of affairs is fraught with the risk of tensions and even conflicts, owing to the strategic importance of energy supplies.

Fossil fuels, are furthermore, responsible for the manmade increase in the carbon-di-oxide content of the earth's atmosphere, with the associated danger of an increase in the greenhouse effect and, as a direct result, global warming of the order of 1º to 4ºC in the next twenty years, which would adversely affect the climate and the environment. Though much uncertainty remains as to the scale of these effects, the risk is great enough to mean that every effort should be made to slow down the increasing "carbonisation" of the atmosphere due to the intensive use of fossil fuels.

Nuclear Power

The main advantage of nuclear power is that it has no effect on the carbon dioxide content of the atmosphere. As it is also cheaper (per energy unit) than hydroelectric or thermal energy, some countries have opted strongly for this way of producing electricity.

Nuclear power is, however, far from being unanimously accepted. Public opinion is very conscious of the lack of candid information and of the safety of nuclear plants, two aspects that have not always been treated, in some countries, with all the necessary care and clarity by the authorities and the operators. The public is also worried about the disposal of long-lasting radioactive wastes, an acute problem to which the experts seem confident that a long-time solution can be found. It would also be a mistake to underestimate the danger of the spread of nuclear arms, even though the main powers are now significantly reducing their arsenals of these weapons. A final point is that only those countries which can afford to make the huge investments required, can put nuclear plants into operation. The investment is offset by the low cost of the fuel but is recouped only in the medium and long term.

Renewable Energy Sources

The ecological movements, which are worried both by global warming and by the real or imagined dangers of nuclear power, would like renewable energy sources to be developed faster than is now the case. These forms of energy at present supply some 18 per cent of total demand, which puts them well ahead of nuclear power.

Technology is moving rapidly forward in this field. These forms of energy are capable of meeting the needs of communities that it would be too expensive to connect to a central grid supply, but despite improved productivity and falling costs, they remain on the whole dearer than the two previous forms. It will be a long time before they can constitute the main source of supply. Other problems that remain to be solved include the major investments required for hydroelectric power stations and the environmental damage caused by the building of dams and wind farms.

We must face the fact that as of now there is no "miralce" energy that is risk-free for humans and their environment and is also cheap and inexhaustible. There is no such thing as absolute security as regards power generation and use, and it will not be possible in the future to do without any of the above-mentioned sources. Energy demand will continue to grow as a result of irreversible technological advances, of the justified demands of the non-industrialised countries, and of population growth that is in any case set to continue for at least the next fifty years.

Some Ethical Principles

A number of imperatives must thus be borne in mind by every individual, every nation and, in particular, the citizens of the industrialised countries. These are: the right of each individual to sufficient sources of energy; our responsibility towards our children and our children's children, protection of the environment; prevention of the potential major risks from the production of energy on a massive scale; the control of costs and the need to carry on with research in all these fields.

Some of these obligations—those relating to population growth, climate change or the disposal of nuclear wastes, for example—are of a very long-term nature, while others—efforts to deal with pollution caused by road transport or chemical waste disposal—are short-term. These differences of time-scale and the various possible interactions between the quantitative and qualitative aspects of the question have to be taken into account in observations of an ethical character such as the following:

- The present situation, wherby nearly one person in four in the world is without access to the energy resources he or she requires, cannot be accepted with resignation. Those with an active role in energy policy-decision-makers, industrialists, research workers and so forth—must ultimately ensure that there exist, and continue to exist, sufficient resources of sufficiently cheap energy for all countries to have access to them, regardless of their geographical or economic situation;
- There should be no pretext for unnecessarily keeping the countries of the South, which urgently need proper infrastructures, on short commons as regards energy use. This is one area where, more than in any other, people need to be informed, so that they can take part in discussion and decision-making on subjects where scientific and technological knowledge is essential;
- Our duty to future generations enjoins us to use energy resources as sparingly and rationally as possible, especially as we know that a major part of these resources may be exhausted in a century or two;
- Even though rapid progress is being made in the exploration of space, we must acknowledge the obvious fact that we have only one Earth and must therefore

preserve and protect it. Since energy production and use may jeopardize our environment, there is an urgent need for appropriate measures to be taken as rapidly and as effectively as possible. The management of nuclear waste and campaigns to combat all forms of pollution arising from energy use constitute unconditional obligations in this connection;

- Whenever massive quantities of nuclear or other forms of energy are produced or transported, e.g. when oil is transported by sea or big dams are built, major risks to life and health ensue. Absolute safety is unattainable, but the various energy authorities are nevertheless under an obligation to issue and enforce appropriate safety regulations;
- Unit cost will continue to be the main factor influencing the choice between different forms of energy. Production costs must be controlled and savings constantly sought if energy supplies are to be available to all;
- Research sometimes seems to have been neglected in work on energy production and consumption, but it is an indispensable duty. Efforts to find new sources of energy and more economical ways of using it must continue.

Further Recommendations

We must keep our eyes open for the early warning signs of potentially dangerous or irreversible situations, and react quickly to them.

Application of the "precautionary principle" remains an unconditional obligation. We must take economic and fiscal measures designed to avert the risks of tension between producers and consumers and to encourage proper control of the resource in question. The tax instrument should be used to redistribute resources between privileged and less privileged groups of the population.

The man and woman in the street and their elected representatives must be informed about everything relating to the production and consumption of every kind of energy. Parliaments should have their own scientific and technological evaluation services, as is the case in certain countries. Projections made on the basis of different economic and demographic hypotheses ought to be regularly updated.

Now it is realised that no form of energy can replace any other form, we must endeavour to preserve the balance between producers and consumers, between rich and poor and between those that are spendthrift and those that are thrifty.

3

Not Yet Fossil Fuel

People were gathering wood for their fires more quickly than it could grow back. In India, wood was being burned 50 per cent faster than replacement trees were growing. Among environmentalists, the perception became widespread that village cooking fires were consuming the Indian forest.

Firewood demand was a minor cause of deforestation. People were mostly using twigs and dead branches for fuel, leaving trees standing. The main perpetrators of deforestation were not women preparing for the evening meal, but farmers clearing land for crops and livestock. To this day, however, the belief persists that fuelwood scarcity drives deforestation. That popular misconception has hampered efforts to address serious fuelwood problems that do exist. While not quite deforesting the globe, these problems are undermining the well-being of millions of people in India.

Until recently, most biomass consumer lived in rural areas. As populations have grown, and the number of trees has diminished, searching for fuelwood has indeed become a demanding task. In some areas of India, for example, collecting firewood was a two-hour task only a generation ago, yet today it is almost an entire day's expedition—every day. That constitutes an enormous erosion of productivity in other kinds of work. And the problem is worsening rapidly.

What makes the situation even more difficult is that fuel-wood problems have now spread from rural areas to the cities. In the 1950s, the cities in India were relatively small, inhabited mainly by those who could afford such "modern" fuels as kerosene, liquefied petroleum gas (LPG), and electricity. But in the past three decades, urban populations have exploded as migrants from the rural areas pour into the cities in search of jobs and higher standards of living.

Despite the availability of the "modern" energy sources to some of the city dwellers, the majority of migrants cannot afford them. Wood remains their fuel. But instead of collecting it, they now must buy it from vendors.

Biomass traders search for wood in communal woodlots, and consequently procure it as a "free" commodity. The price of the wood, which represents only the transport costs and trader's markups, excludes the production and replacement costs at the expense of rural people and the natural resource base. After decades of woodland exploitation in some areas of India, the shortage of firewood in rural areas has become so severe that villagers are compelled to use cow-dung, dried leaves, and grass for fuel. The fragile soils of the farmlands are thus denied essential nutrients and organic matter.

Villagers are working hard to reduce the exploitation of their resource-base by the urban entrepreneurs. For example, in a village not far from the capital city of Delhi, residents decided to charge traders for wood taken from their communal land. Extension agents were brought in to train the villagers in negotiating wood prices, maintaining accounts, and establishing an agro-forestry project. The revenue from wood sales is now used by the villagers to plant trees that will not only provide fuel for their personal use and for sale, but can be used for other purposes such as construction.

Dependence on wood for fuel is not just a challenge to economic sustainability, but also a threat to Indians health. In the homes of low-income families, where traditional wood stoves are widely used for cooking, adequate ventilation is often lacking. These stoves require large quantities of wood, are unable to retain heat for prolonged periods, and send much of the fuel up in smoke. Inhaled by women as they cook, the smoke has been identified as a major cause of respiratory problems such as bronchitis, and of damaged eyesight.

Improved wood and charcoal stoves are now for sale in India. Because they require significantly smaller quantities of firewood or charcoal, they are successfully curbing the wood demand, and hence promoting biomass conservation.

In the cities, as vendors travel longer distances into the hinterland in search of wood, and the transportation costs increase, more of the market is shifting to charcoal, which is easier to transport and more convenient to use in cramped urban quarters. However, widespread use of charcoal puts even greater stress on the environment because conversion from wood to charcoal requires twice as much timber to yield the same cooking energy.

In addition, once the conversion, transportation and combustion processes have been accounted for, charcoal emerges as one of the leading producers of carbon-di-oxide—the most prevalent greenhouse gas. A meal cooked with charcoal produces three times more carbon-di-oxide than the same meal cooked with wood. On the other hand, charcoal can be made into a more efficient fuel by producing it in kilns that retain a higher proportion of the energy content within the charcoal. And the amount of charcoal used can be reduced by the use of more efficient charcoal stoves, which control airflow to the fuel and are insulated to minimize heat loss.

Looking for alternatives to fuelwood and its charcoal derivative, a number of communities are experimenting with solar box cookers and biogas digesters, both of which use renewable sources of energy and are pollutant-free and energy-efficient. The solar cookers and the digestors have been successful on a small and localised scale. The new methods have not been used on a big scale because of the high initial costs along with a variety of cultural biases and superstitions. For example, preparing and cooking food is an evening social activity, and solar cookers have to be used during the day. Biogas digestors are similarly constrained, since in some cultures the use of human and livestock waste, as fuel is unacceptable.

The fuelwood crisis is complicated one, and the easy, large-scale solutions that were originally recommended, such as the establishment of peri-urban plantations to increase woodfuel supplies, evidently will do little, if anything, to alleviate the problem. However, over the years, through mistakes and project failures, a few useful lessons have been learned. One such lesson—counter-intuitive though it may seem to many environmentalists is that since biomass fuels will continue to play a major role for years to come, greater emphasis needs to be placed on finding ways to increase the woodfuel supply. Farmers, for example, can be encouraged to plant trees that will provide not only fuel but other products such as fruits, fodder, and lumber. And when the new high-efficiency stoves are made more widely available, the demand for trees will be reduced—even as their supply is increased.

4

Population Growth and Urbanisation

The world's cities are growing far faster than its population. Indeed, aside from the growth of population itself, urbanisation is the dominant demographic trend of the half-century now ending. In 1950, 750 million of the world's people lived in cities. By 1996, this had at least tripled, to more than 2.6 billion. The number projected to live in cities by 2050, some 6.5 billion people, exceeds world population today.

Urbanisation on anything like the scale that we know today is historically quite recent. In 1800, only one city, London, had a million people. Today, 326 cities have at least that many people. And there are 14 mega cities, those with 10 million or more residents. Tokyo is the largest, at 27 million. Mexico city is second, at 17 million. New York city and Sao Paulo are close behind, with 16 million each. Rounding out the list in descending size are Bombay (15 million), Shanghai (14), Los Angeles (12), Calcutta (12), Buenos Aires (12), Beijing (11), Osaka (11), Lagos (10), Rio de Janeiro (10), and Delhi (10).

The rate of growth of cities in industrial countries during the first century or so of the Industrial Revolution was relatively slow. Today's cities are growing much faster. It took London 130 years to get from 1 million to 8 million. Mexico city made this jump in just 30 years.

Measured in annual growth, some cities, such as Lagos, Nigeria, are growing at 5 per cent a year; Bombay is growing at nearly 4 per cent. The world's urban population as a whole is growing by just over 1 million people each week. This urban growth is fed by natural increase of urban populations, by net migration from the countryside, and by villages, or towns expanding to the point where they become cities or they are absorbed by the spread of existing cities.

During the early stages of industrialisation, urbanisation was largely in response to the pull of employment opportunities in cities. More recently, however, the movement from countryside to city has been more the result of rural push than of urban pull. It is a reflection of the lack of opportunity in the countryside as already small plots of land are divided and then divided again with each passing generation, until they become so small that people can no longer make a living from them.

Historically, cities and the surrounding countryside had a symbolic relationship, with the latter supplying food and raw materials in exchange for manufactured products. Today, cities are tied much more to each other and to the global economy. The food and fuel that once came from the surrounding countryside now often comes from distant corners of the planet.

As societies urbanize, the use of basic resources, such an energy and water rises. In traditional rural societies, for example, people live on the land and thus do not need to travel to work. But once they migrate to cities, commuting becomes the rule, not the exception. In villages, most of the food that is consumed is produced locally, requiring little energy for processing, packaging, and transportation; once people move into cities, on the other hand, virtually all their food must be brought in. In a village where residents typically draw their water from a central well and carry it to their homes, water use in necessarily limited. But when villagers move to urban high-rise apartment buildings with indoor plumbing, replete with showers and flush toilets, water consumption soars.

The ecology of cities is a continuing challenge to city managers simply because cities require the concentration of huge quantities of water, food, energy and raw materials. The waste products must then be dispersed or the city will become uninhabitable. As cities become larger, the disposal of residential and industrial wastes becomes ever more challenging.

Partly as a result of the mounting pressure for people to migrate to cities, the growth in urban populations is far out-stripping the availability of basic services, such as water, sewerage, transportation, and electricity. As a result, life in urban shantytowns is plagued by poverty, pollution, congestion, homelessness, and unemployment.

Since the beginning of the Industrial Revolution, the terms of trade between countryside and city have favoured the latter simply because cities control the scarce resources in development, namely capital and technology. But if the price of food rises in the years ahead, as now seems likely, the terms of trade could shift, favouring the countryside. If in the new world of the twenty-first century the scarce resources are land and water, those controlling them could have the upper hand in determining rural/urban terms of trade.

This aside, if recent trends continue, within the next several years more than half of us will be living in cities—making the world more urban than rural for the first time in history. We will have become an urban species, far removed from our hunter-gatherer origins.

5

Innovative Milieus—Cities

Cities provide the local bases for international linkages. This is where the virtual worlds of highly specified communication networks are anchored. Complicating matters, globalisation and urbanisation have certain features in common. They challenge the existing order, constantly frustrate planning and emphasise plurality. Tension is the norm, cannot be avoided, and must, therefore, be handled constructively. Not coincidentally, however, cities posses civilising qualities: their very existence depends on reducing levels of violence.

Globalisation and urbanisation are two trends characterising the present. These two phenomena are closely linked because globalisation means that global networks emerge, which have their nodes in cities. The networks are heterogeneous, frequently based on competition and provide the stuff of which conflicts are made. At stake are cash flows, transnational companies, international civil society, migrant groups, religious communities, multilateral politics and cultural interdependencies. Nor should one forget the challenges of organised transnational crime or global terrorism. This is where global interests seek to maximize profits, but also where local grassroots and civil society develop new claims to assert rights to liveable urban space.

Global Cities

Global cities are defined as locations, which support international networking. They are under particular pressure and it sometimes even seems doubtful whether a global city can be treated as a single, coherent entity at all. There is a prevailing trend towards fragmentation because of the permanent competition of various norms and values, identities and social realities. This trend is exacerbated when populations organise in various local networks. On the other hand, the global networks use virtual habitats with far-reaching rules of largely homogenous quality. In this sense, financial markets, for example, command their own virtual cities—as do heroin or cocaine dealing. Such virtual contexts, are, in turn, locally embedded in real cities. They dominate some neighbourhood but hardly affect others.

The traditional concept of "world cities" is passe. The notion referred to command centres with transnational significance and cosmopolitan culture. However, the hierarchy of various urban functions is no longer stable or permanent. Whereas the world city was viewed as control centre of the modern world system, the global city is integrated in distinctive global networks, none of which can automatically be assumed to be dominant, structuring or even yielding to the national government. Rather, we are dealing with distinct realities which are compatible only to various degrees and sometimes even incompatible. Global cities are characterised by confusion, because their various realities can no longer be integrated into a single system.

Global cities, moreover, contribute to our planet's environmental crisis. The size of airports is a good indicator of how global any particular agglomeration has become. On the other hand, air travel is a major, unregulated source of green house emissions. Petrochemical fuels, on which most cities thrive, are the world market's core commodity.

In addition, large urban agglomerations are often located on the most fertile land and thus there extension reduces agricultural production. Every urban centre depends on food from outside, stimulating not only traffic but also intensive production in the hinterland, which in turn, has also become international. Afterall the pineapples on display in

Frankfurt's supermarkets do not grow in Germany, nor can the citizens of Toronto consume domestically produced lemons and oranges. It must be considered, however, how sustainability of natural resources would be challenged, if instead of population concentrations, we had highly overpopulated rural region in need of adequate infrastructure.

Cities have always served diverse cultures as arenas for encounter and exchange and accordingly, also as arenas of conflict. This applies to contemporary global cities more than ever before. Nevertheless, they are more than just articulation nodes of transnational networks. In view of the fact that the world is divided into territorial states, cities also belong to national political systems, for which they normally play distinct and decisive roles. Fashion, trends and other types of societal change have always originated from cities. Modern representative democracy was born of the cities—key historical events such as the Storming of the Bastille and the Boston Tea Party provide the evidence. On the other hand, state institutions are based in cities, from the national tax administration to judicial authority. A further aspect is social starification, because a nation's elite usually lives in the major cities.

Of course, not all of a city's people and communities are integrated in global networks. Social contexts with specific local histories, which different from the realisations of global networks, are equally relevant. In the cities local, national and global phenomena inter-relate. Executive managers with worldwide spheres of activity depend on their maids who—particularly, but not only, in poor countries—may hardly ever leave the household.

Traditionally, the urbanisation debate revolved around the experience of those nations that industrialised early. Empirical research normally looks at the aglomerations in Europe, North America and Japan, where the respective histories have national characteristics. In contrast, the development of Singapore, Kuala Lumpur or Jakarta resulted from colonialism. The dynamism of their growth was, from the outset, associated with glob ıl networks.

To this day, Third World Cities tend to be much more diverse than most OECD cities. While nationalism served as a central mechanism to integrate the urban populations in Europe in the 19th century, similar efforts in the colonial cities were regarded as a threat and suppressed as effectively as possible. Consequently, it is still common to find urban cultures in which rural places of origin define identities. People relate to their "homeland", which may be thousands of kilometres away and which some may not visit in their lifetime, rather than with the immediate neighbours they meet everyday.

All cities have their own history resulting in particular features. Urbanistion becomes specific in each city, but is likely to also affect other regions, because cities never exist in isolation. They always belong to systems of various corresponding centres, because population groups pursue the same interests, or, at least, related interests. This typically is expressed in architecture, with the result that, even today, one can still find traces of the Northern Italian Renaissance in small towns of other countries.

Moreover, urbanisation implies a civilising process. To exist in the long term, cities must curb violence, despite the diverse nature of their populations and their conflicting interests. Wherever that is not done successfully, cities become irrelevant fast. The connection between civilising and urbanism is based on two pillars. These are firstly the public sphere and political deliberation and, secondly, something I have described elsewhere as "locality". Locality ensures social control through personal contacts and interlinking institutions. It is not about communities or districts, but networks of relationships which are integrated through various activities. Locality arises from initiative and self organisation and can hardly be orchestrated by administrations. Locality and public sphere complement each other. Otherwise, self-created and self-regulated interactions could not persist under the pressure of real estate speculation, official town planning, and other dominant societal forces.

The World Bank holds a similar view. Its Urban Peace Programme zeroes in on strategies to reduce violence. The focus is on supporting local communities in an effort to increase "social capital". In a similar vein, violence erodes social capital, as it reduces trust and cooperation within formal and informal social organisations that are critical for a society to function.

Planning Paralysis

The rapid growth of many cities makes building social capital particularly important. There must be scope for creative and cooperative improvisation, because local authorities are often strikingly overburdened. The enormous size of mega-cities with several million inhabitants makes it clear that comprehensive control and even planning are impossible. In many cases, civil servants do not even notice that new slums have formed within a few years, which may easily have more inhabitants than large towns. Such developments make the demand for better planning obsolete from the outset. Too often, we do not really know what makes mega-cities tick.

It is clear that private enterprise steps in where profits are attractive. This applies to local business but also to multinational corporations. Well-known examples are provided in the construction industry, building homes, offices, factories and roads. But schools and hospitals are also operated privately. Without private bus, and in some places, even rail companies, traffic would collapse completely. Lucrative mobile telephone markets are expanding, where the conventional fixed line telephone network has been overburdened for decades. Electricity and water supply offer opportunities, both for multinational companies smelling profit and for slum dwellers attempting to tap utility services for free.

It is not uncommon for clashes to occur with city authorities. What official regulations demand often makes little sense to the firm engaged or the people affected. Influential persons are often involved in the private companies, which helps to avoid official rules or to have them re-written. Whether corruption takes place or formal decision processes are adhered to, may make surprisingly little difference on the ground. Typically very little attention is paid to the needs of poor people.

Nevertheless, urban life offers opportunities for economic, political and cultural participation even for marginalised people. This is what leads to rural-urban migration in the first place. Admittedly, it also means tough competition for housing space. There is ever-increasing demand for shelter. At the same time, the public and private sector are neither interested in, nor in a position to fulfill the right to an 'adequate shelter. The poor urban population can improve its fate only in the slums and often only using its own initiative—such as through locally supported microfinance schemes to get legal access to land.

This kind of societal creativity in initiative and self-organisation is not limited to the production of housing. It is also visible in petty trading and the informal sector, which blossom in economic niches and continues to discover new niches. Among the fields of activity are waste recycling, domestic services or, of course, drug peddling, "Innovative milieus" are not only found in business high-rises, universities and research institutes. They are also prolific in slums markets and even on garbage dumps.

Initiative, self-organisation and social creativity have political consequences. Communal self-determination and the building up of local organisations depend on democratic principles. Formal participation is relevant—but so is scope for informal improvisation. The relevance of grassroots activity is one reason for totalitarian and authoritarian regimes always looking at cities with great scepticism. Revolts and protest movements normally start in the urban centres. How political challenges are dealt with, on the other hand, sets precedents, which define what is normal and to be expected. This is institution building in practical terms. It happens spontaneously and unplanned—with long term consequences far beyond the city limits. Periods of rapid growth, moreover, are particularly critical because they are, by definition, times of rapid change.

Conclusion

Things often happen in unplanned and disorderly ways in cities and agglomerations. Especially in poor countries, the living conditions are often anything but idylic. Nevertheless, there is no alternative in the development process but to build on this difficult foundation. Inspite of all the dirt, misery and hardship, urban environments offer prospects not only of survival but also of participation, democratic modernisation and civilisation (in the basic sense of reducing violent interaction). That people are flocking into the cities proves that these places attractive in spite of their dismal slums, overflowing drains and congested traffic. It is telling that it is so rare, in poor countries, to see anyone return to their rural homes for good.

Globalisation accelerates the dynamics described above, while urbanisation is, at the same time providing the base for making international networks ever more important. Both trends are interrelated. They imply that city life is gaining relevance in economic, political and cultural terms with the influence of specific urban settings potentially spreading far beyond the borders of the nation-state, without, however, making urbanisation more predictable or even more amendable to planning. On the contrary: the potential for conflict is growing.

❄ ❄ ❄

6

Cities Residents to the Rescue

In the next ten years, the number of people living in cities will rise to around 3.3 billion. Tokyo already has a population of 27 million, Sao Paulo (Brazil) 16.4 million, and Bombay 15 million. World Bank forecasts show as much as 80 per cent of the developing countries economic growth occurring in the cities and major conurbations.

There are both positive and negative aspects to these developments. At each stage in the history of urbanisation, environmental conditions in cities were improved dramatically. The process was often slow, but over time, many epidemic diseases have been controlled, the supply of clean water and the removal of wastes have become routine, the risks of fire have been contained and standards of comfort and cleanliness have risen to unprecedented levels. Cities could not have become as large and as numerous as they are now if environmental conditions had remained unchanged.

In a curious way, the pollution that cities suffer is largely due to their wealth. The rich consume a great deal more energy, water, building materials and other goods than the poor and thus produce much more waste. This is what is happening, in the cities where rapid industrialisation is taking place—only the rich enjoy the benefits of piped water and refuse collection.

Increasingly Insanitary Conditions

There is another, often tragic, aspect to this situation. The poorest of the poor are reduced to living in outer-edge shantytowns in extremely insanitary conditions and lacking the resources to deal with the problem, the city as a whole has to endure congestion and air and water pollution. Some towns and cities are expanding at a rate of over 7 per cent a year, municipal sanitation departments are no longer able to cope, and it is estimated that as many as 30 per cent of the population are without running water.

In many of the world's major cities runaway population growth, an epidemic of Aids and rising social tensions have been combined in the last few years with a steep drop in incomes. The population living on the outer edges of the cities continues to grow apace, hundreds of thousands of people are without running water and 15 per cent of them without sanitation of any sort. Various voluntary bodies and non-governmental organisations have got together, often successfully.

Water and the Environmental Crisis

One key problem concerns the availability of clean water. Some progress has been achieved as a result of the International Drinking Water Supply and Sanitation Decade, but in 1994 at least 220 million people still lacked a source of drinking water near their homes. In some cases, communities of 500 or more inhabitants are served by a single tap. In some towns, communal taps function for only a few hours a day, so that people cannot build up sufficient reserves of water for their personal needs if it takes too long to fetch or if the water has to be carried long distances.

As there are no proper sanitation measures, the disadvantaged members of the population have to drink dirty water, fish in polluted streams and eat vegetables that have been grown by the side of refuse tips.

A further major problem arises from the three-fold harmful impact of cities on the environment: urban development on agricultural land, the extraction and exhaustion of natural resources and the dumping of refuse.

Growing pressure on coastal regions, where nearly a billion people now live, is doing serious damage to the marine environment. Development activities pose a threat to nearly half the world's coasts.

Towns originally offered people a place of refuge, of mutual help and culture. According to nineteenth-century town-planning theorists, they should supply all human needs. They were supposed to be the very stuff of civilisation. That was not to be, and therefore whenever the authorities throw in their hands, dismayed by the scale of the problems and lacking the political will, money or resources to cope with them, personal initiatives are those most likely to succeed.

7

Sustainable Cities

Today almost one half of the world's population lives in cities. The world's cities are growing by one million people each week. Cities today play a significant role in development. They continue to attract migrants from rural areas because they enable people to advance socially and economically. Cities offer significant economies of scale in the provision of jobs, housing and services, and are important centres of productivity and social development.

However, the stress of this rapid urban population growth is often overwhelming. The long list of afflictions includes urban poverty rates of up to 60 per cent. Despite growing investments, more than one-third of the urban population live in substandard housing. Forty per cent of urban dwellers do not have access to safe drinking water or adequate sanitation. Primarily due to a rapid growth and a deteriorating urban environment, at least 600 million people in human settlements (cities, towns and villages) already live in health and life threatening situations, and almost 50 per cent of these are children.

The high rate of urban population growth in most regions has led to common problems: congestion, lack of funds to provide basic services, a shortage of adequate housing and declining infrastructure, to name a few.

While these problems are occurring in urban areas, cities still have an important role to play in protecting the global environment in the face of rapid urban population growth. Agricultural and livestock production in rural areas are pushing farther and farther into ecologically fragile regions and cannot support growing population. The finite land and water resources make it imperative that human settlements be carefully planned. Indeed, sustainable urbanisation will ease the pressures caused by encroachment on fragile natural habitats.

India's cities offer a bewildering sight to any visitor: the congestion caused by rapid population growth and a continuing rural-urban drift often leads to conditions which defy all rules of orders, hygiene and environmental safety. Inadequate leadership, corruption and mismanagement have a harmful effect on the physical, environmental, social and ethical structures of cities in India.

Millions of people live in inadequate conditions—without piped water, electricity, security of land tenure, access to roads or health facilities. The means available for production and financing of housing and urban infrastructure are too limited to meet basic needs.

Reducing Poverty and Creating Jobs

Urban poverty is rising at an alarming pace, especially among women. The informal economic sector—which makes a substantial contribution to the delivery of services, production of goods, building of infrastructure and housing construction—often provides the only opportunity for the urban poor to make a living.

Local informal housing construction, for example, generates up to 20 per cent more jobs than high-cost construction. Street hawking, waste recycling and food production are primary sources of income among the urban poor and are illustrative of the creativity of survival strategies.

However, the informal sector itself is often highly exploitative and fails to raise people's economic development beyond mere subsistence. Larger economic strategies and more participatory urban planning approaches that take stock of local skills, technologies and materials are required to generate new and better-paying job opportunities in cities and towns.

Incorporating Environmental Concerns

In 1992 the Rio Conference on Environment and Development designed the Agenda 21 Programme of Action to help save a planet endangered by environmental neglect and plagued by poverty and underdevelopment. Most of the goals agreed to in Rio can become reality only through local action in cities where environmental threats are increasing. Again, it is the urban poor who are particularly endangered by environmental degradation and pollution. The world's Agenda 21 will fail if the city's environmental agenda (population, inadequate sanitation, water supply and waste management) is not addressed. This is being recognised by local authorities all over the world.

Sustainable development in the twenty first century will to a large degree, depend upon how cities, towns and villages everywhere interact with the environment and utilize natural resources.

Increasing Awareness of Gender Issues

Women and men use and experience cities differently, according to their roles, responsibilities and access to resources. For example, when basic services are lacking in a settlement, more often than not it is women who take on responsibilities such as water collection and refuse disposal. Women often have unequal access to resources such as property, credit, training and technology. All of these factors must be addressed urgently, as they make it harder for women to improve their living standards and those of their children.

Disaster Mitigation Relief and Reconstruction

As cities become large and more densely populated, they become increasingly vulnerable to natural and man-made disasters such as earthquake, floods, industrial hazards, epidemics, civil strife and wars. Poor people are forced to live in the most exposed, dangerous and cramped conditions; in flood-prone areas, on steep hillsides or near polluted streams and waste dumps. As a result, they are most likely to lose their homes or their lives when disasters occur. Better planning, access to affordable urban land, and improved construction methods can reduce the extent of catastrophes.

These successful and sustainable approaches to poverty eradication; managing the urban environment; providing access to land, shelter and finance; empowering women and men; and many other issues will have to be documented and disseminated widely.

8

Towards Healthy Cities

More than a third of the urban population in developing world live in housing of such poor quality with such inadequate provision for water, sanitation, drainage, garbage collection and health care that their health is constantly under threat. But, properly planned, cities can be safe and healthy.

In the cities of India, it is common for one child in three to die before the age of five and for virtually all infants, children and adults who survive to have disease burdens many times higher than they should.

Diarrhoea, tuberculosis and respiratory infections (each among the largest causes of death) are generally much increased by over-crowding. Many accidental injuries happen when there are three or more persons living in each small room in shelters made of flammable materials and there is little chance of providing occupants (especially children) with protection from open fires or stoves.

But cities also include some of the India's safest and most healthy neighbourhoods. High densities allow much lower costs for supplying each household with piped, treated water supplies and most forms of health, educational and emergency services.

Sanitation and drainage may be costly in cities, as complex systems are needed to cope with high densities and large population concentrations but city households can generally afford to pay more—and are prepared to do so if they get a good service.

Cities may be considered ecologically unsustainable because of high consumption and waste levels but well planned and managed cities can combine high living standards with remarkably low levels of energy consumption, resource use and wastes. The concentration of people and production creates many more possibilities of collecting and recycling wastes and for walking, bicycling and a high quality public transport.

For many, city-life is one of excessive workloads and drudgery, yet cities remain centres of culture—including the visual and decorative arts, music, dance, theatre and literature. Most cities have a large reserve of young people on whose initiative and energy they could draw to improve conditions—yet most such people find that their cities offer them little hope and little prospect of employment. If cities have such potential to provide healthy, stimulating and valued places to live and work for all age groups, why do so few achieve this?

Supporting Change

Much of the explanation is the lack of 'good governance'. Good governance in any city means encouragement and support from all levels of government for a great range of investments of capital, expertise and time by individuals, households, communities, voluntary organisations and NGOs—as well as private enterprises. In most cities in India, the total value of investments made by people in their own homes and neighbourhoods exceeds many times the total value of capital investments made by city and municipal authorities. Yet governments and aid agencies usually ignore (or deem illegal) most such efforts.

Most households who want their own home cannot afford to purchase one—or at least one that is legal. They cannot obtain housing loans so the cost of the house purchase can be spread over a number of years—as they cannot meet the (usually) inappropriate conditions set by banks or housing finance institutions. If they turn to building their own home—as most do—they have to occupy or purchase the site illegally. They often have to build on dangerous sites—in floodplains or on slopes with frequent landslides or mudslides—as the cost of safer sites is too high.

Even if they can qualify, for a housing loan; most such loans are for finished houses, not for incremental construction. And even when they have developed their own home and neighbourhood into a viable residential area, governments usually refuse to provide these with roads, water supplies, drains and other essential infrastructure, because they are 'illegal'.

What would cities look like today if governments had supported these individual and community efforts by ensuring that land, building materials, credit and technical advice were as cheap and readily available as possible? Or if government-community partnerships had been formed to, at least, improve water supply, sanitation, drainage and health care.

These work within what is often called the 'social economy'—the great variety of initiatives and actions that are organised and controlled locally and that are not profit-oriented. The social economy includes the work of citizen groups, resident's associations, street or barrio clubs, youth clubs, and parent associations that support local schools. It includes many voluntary groups that provide services for the elderly, the physically disabled or other individuals in need of social. It often includes many initiatives that make cities safer and more fun-helping provide supervised play space, sport and recreational opportunities for children and youth. It may provide formal or informal supervision or maintenance of parks, squares, and other public spaces.

The social economy not only 'gets things done' but also creates a dense fabric of relationships that allows citizens to work together in identifying and acting on local problems.

Its value to a 'healthy city' is enormous, even if it is often forgotten by governments and international agencies.

The capacity of city authorities to govern is not the same as the capacity to invest, since these authorities can do much to encourage and support the social economy. City authorities can often greatly increase the supply and reduce the cost of land for housing by changing inappropriate regulations, streamlining planning and land use control, procedure and making better use of publicly owned land.

City authorities should also have the main role in enforcing legislation on, air and water pollution and occupational health and safety. This does not require large investments by public authorities, but it can do much to improve health and the quality of life in a city. Good governance also means managing competing claims and finding common ground between enterprises, trade unions and residents about what should be done to make the city more healthy.

Achieving a healthy city needs a representative political system through which the priorities of citizens and businesses can influence policies and actions. Democratic structures remain among the best checks on the misallocation of resources by city and municipal governments. Actively involving a wide range of local groups in developing 'city governance' helps ensure that the different priorities of a wide range of groups are addressed.

The key issue is not so much identifying what should be done to achieve more healthy cities. This is well known. It is identifying how it should be done, especially how governments and international agencies can support a vast range of activities by individuals, households and communities that help build and maintain healthy cities—which to date they have ignored or even (for many governments) repressed.

❋ ❋ ❋

9

Cities at the Forefront

The rapid growth of cities in the developing world puts them in the forefront of the struggle for improved living standards and protection of the environment. Since 1950 the urban population has more than tripled, from just over 750 million to about 3 billion by 2030 some 5 billion people will live in cities. In the developing world the urban population is projected to double from 1.9 billion in 2000 to be just under 4 billion by 2030.

World-wide, about three-fourths of all current population growth is urban. Cities are gaining an estimated 55 million people per year—over 1 million new residents every week from in-migration and natural population increase within cities. In developing countries many cities are growing two or three times faster than population growth for the country as a whole. As cities grow ever lager, their impact on the environment grows exponentially.

The Rise of Megacities

The UN coined the term megacities in 1970s to describe cities with 10 million or more residents. As recently as 1975 there were only five megacities world-wide. Currently, there are 19 megacities, of which 15 are in developing countries. By 2015 the number of megacities will grow to 23 which is explained in Table 9.1. Megacities have captured public interest because cities this large are unprecedented in history

and because of the popular perception that human well-being will decline in such dense concentration of people.

Table 9.1: Megacities of the World

Cities with 10 Million or More Inhabitants, 1975, 2000 and 2015 (Population in Millions)

City-1975	*Population*	*City-2000*	*Population*	*City-2015*	*Population*
Tokyo	19.8	Tokyo	26.4	Tokyo	26.4
New York	15.9	Mexico City	18.1	Bombay	26.1
Shanghai	11.4	Bombay	18.1	Lagos	23.2
Mexico City	11.2	Sao Paulo	17.8	Dhaka	21.1
Sao Paulo	10.0	Shanghai	17.0	Sao Paulo	20.4
		New York	16.6	Karachi	19.2
		Lagos	13.4	Mexio city	19.2
		Los Angeles	13.1	Shanghai	19.1
		Calcutta	12.9	New York	17.4
		Buenos Aires	12.6	Jakarta	17.3
		Dhaka	12.3	Calcutta	17.3
		Karachi	11.8	Delhi	16.8
		Delhi	11.7	Metro Manila	14.8
		Jakarta	11.0	Los Angeles	14.1
		Osaka	11.0	Buenos Aires	14.1
		Metro Manila	10.9	Cairo	13.8
		Beijing	10.8	Istanbul	12.5
		Rio de Janeiro	10.6	Beijing	12.3
		Cairo	10.6	Rio de Janeiro	11.9
				Osaka	11.0
				Tianjin	10.7
				Hyderabad	10.5
				Bangkok	10.1

Source: UN Population Division, March 2000 (p: 239).

Millions of people move from the countryside to the city to seek a better life, but they often find that their lives become more difficult. In many cities 25 per cent to 30 per cent of the urban population live in poor shanty towns or squatter settlements, or they live on the streets. Of Rio de Janeiro's 10.6 million residents, for example, 4 million live in squatter settlements and shanty towns, some perched precariously on step hillsides. Nevertheless, cities in developing countries continue to attract more and more people.

Cities occupy only 2 per cent of the world's land surface, but city populations have a disproportionate impact on the environment. For example, London requires rough 60 times its land area to supply its 9 million residents with food and forest products. Because commerce and trade have spread dramatically in recent years, city residents consume resources not just from surrounding areas, but, increasingly, from around the world. Urban areas also export their wastes and pollutants, affecting environmental and health conditions far from the cities themselves.

What Can be Done?

In the long run, slowing population growth would help ease the pressure on cities, buying time to make improvements in technology. Municipalities also can take a number of steps now—building better transportation systems, promoting recycling and encouraging water conservation.

Public Transportation: One of the best investments that cities can make—both environmental and economic is an efficient mass transportation system. In many cities people waste great amounts of time and fuel going nowhere because traffic congestion is severe. In many urban areas vehicular exhausts account for 50 per cent to 70 per cent of polluting emissions, curbing the number of motor vehicles by offering transportation alternatives would save energy and reduce pollution. Some cities for example, Amsterdam and Copenhagen—have helped ease the transportation crisis by creating special traffic lanes for bicycles and by urging bicycle use.

Recycling: Recycling mountains of urban waste into new resources makes sense both environmentally and economically. Recycling saves natural resources and reduces the amount of trash deposited in landfills or dumped into rivers, lakes and the ocean. Also, for every million tons of solid waste, about 1,600 recycling jobs could be created in developed and developing countries alike.

Water Conservation: Urbanisation dramatically increases per capita freshwater use, as millions of households gain access to piped water, as industry increases and as large-scale irrigated agriculture replaces subsistence farming. Cities everywhere need to adopt water conservation measures.

10

City Politics

A Voice for the Poor

By 2020 the world's urban population will rise by almost 1.5 billion. Cities and towns house a growing proportion of poor people, partly because of the increased share of urban population of the total but also because economic recession and adjustment policies often hit poorer urban residents the hardest. Cities are associated with economic growth and wealth generation and yet inequality is high. Poor people generally live in substandard conditions, may not benefit from job creation, and suffer high levels of pollution, crime and violence.

How can city governments cope with the challenges of population growth and increased global economic competition, and meet the needs of poor residents/is urban governance responsive to the needs of the poor? Are the agencies responsible for city government, especially the municipalities, addressing poor people's needs? Are NGOs and people's organisations playing a greater role in service delivery? Or is their role one of advocacy and lobbying? If so, how do they relate to the formal political system? Can governments fulfil their responsibilities, including poverty reduction? How can the well-being of poor urban governance institutions priorities their needs? In assessing the responsiveness of city government to poor people, three key questions are addressed:

How Can the Poor Influence the Agenda of the Institutions of Urban Governance?

The influence of poor residents on decision-making is controlled, in part, by the formal political system. Democratisation gives people a vote. However, this vote means more when elected representative depend on the political support of poor people—where they are a majority, or are well organised, or where there is a ward-based system. If poor people are organised enough, to articulate their needs and demand a fair share of urban resources. NGOs can help poor groups organise better and provide support for networking.

Where poor people are not organised it does not mean they are politically powerless. Poor people in this situation, however, are prey to the disadvantages of patronage and unlikely to be included in formal consultative processes. For an electoral system to be truly responsive, specific mechanisms and channels, such as consultative and participatory processes at city and sub-city levels, are needed to complement representative democracy. Athough, these channels do not necessarily include the poorest or make a marked difference to resource allocation, pro-poor decisions are unlikely without them.

How Can Cities Finance their Activities and Reduce Poverty?

Democratisation has not, in many countries brought allocation of financial resources or the revenue-raising capacity for local governments to fulfil their responsibilities. The responsiveness of city governments to poor people's needs thus depends, on whose voices are heard in the arenas of political decision-making. Responsiveness also depends on how available financial resources are allocated and how the programmes they finance are designed. There is scope, for city governments to increase property and business revenues, and to borrow for capital investment. Whether increased financial resources benefit poor people depends on how the demands of external investors and creditors are reconciled with the demands of poor residents; the willingness of politicians and officials to address the distributive implications of existing and planned spending; and efficient transparent financial management. If funds are made available to sub-city levels of government or if expenditure can be influenced by ward councilors, the funds might then be used to meet the priorities of poor residents.

What are the Necessities of Urban Living and How Can Access to Then be Ensured?

An Adequate Income: Work opportunities should be the top priority. City governments can, however, support the urban economy in general and the economic activities of the poor in particular. Firstly they can ensure that the basic services are efficiently provided. Secondly city governments can refrain from activities that destroy the assets and livelihoods of the poor, especially eviction of informal settlements and micro-enterprises. Savings and credit schemes can be more appropriately organised at a community level and supported by NGOs.

Land Ownership is a common aspiration for poor households. A home with secure tenure (not necessarily title) provides security, an appreciating asset, access to services, and a base for economic activities. Increasing the opportunities for poor households to gain access to a well-located plot of land is an important component of any poverty reduction strategy. Many never fulfil their dream and the needs of those who cannot, or do not wish to become home owners should not be neglected, however.

Local government is potentially more responsive to poor residents than are central government agencies, although this depends on the balance of political power and bureaucratic perceptions. The limited ability of the public sector to secure benefits for the poor from public-private partnerships in land development, suggest that more informal arrangements and the involvement of CSOs may be better ways forward.

Environmental Services: Land alone will not reduce poverty but must be linked to a healthy living environment—a package of appropriate and affordable environmental services, such as public transport, water and sanitation, solid waste collection, and energy for cooking and lighting. Rather than discussing appropriate standards, detailed issues of financing and affordability or how continued provision can be assured for each of these services, the research focused on how far decision making channels mechanisms and partnership arrangements ensure that providers are responsive to the needs and priorities of poor residents.

Collaborative planning and decision-making arrangements are one promising alternative, despite the current shortcomings of participatory budgeting. For responsiveness to the poor to be built in to such processes, local bureaucrats need to change their attitudes and working practices. Is it possible and acceptable for poor people to have to rely on their own resources their households and networks—resources that are very limited? Informal networks and links can, however, provide mutual support and access to politicians and bureaucrats, community associations thought not always present, inclusive or transparent, can play an important role in articulating poor residents views and in organising self-help activities. There is scope for formal representative community organisations, for informal links between peoples' organsiations and the power structures, and for networking between people's groups. NGOs can play an important role in developing the capacity of community organisations and in facilitating networking. Where NGOs play a role in service delivery. However, there is a danger that the resulting close relationship with local government detracts from their ability to empower poor people and challenge inappropriate policies. City governments, it is clear, cannot cope with the challenges of population and economic growth and respond to the needs of poor people alone. Only in alliance with other actors is there some hope that poverty can be overcome. For CSOs, many of which were forged during struggles for democratisation, this implies moving beyond confrontation to engagement. To form alliances between CSOs and city governments that put the interests of the poor first, poor people must be able to exercise their political rights.

11

Heating-up Environmental Education and Communication

Worldwide environmental issues ranging from the hazardous waste in your backyard to ozone depletion far away in the atmosphere can threaten our planet and compromise our quality of life. The positive and negative effects of environmental interactions are just beginning to be better understood and addressed. Within this context, environmental education and communication have a remarkable opportunity to accelerate understanding and to mobilise national and community participation in change.

Communication because it is the exchange of information. In social programmes, its effectiveness depends on assessing audience needs and taking into account the social, cultural and economic aspects of a problem as well as the quality of education messages and materials.

Education because it involves learning—learning how to think about an issue and its solution; how to acquire and refine skills for solving problems; how to transfer what is learned from situation to situation.

In social programmes, communication and education together lead to increased public participation in problem-solving and in activities which promote change. The participation of many individuals over time can lead to changed expectations for individual behaviour and institutional practices.

The process of communication and education together might be thought of as the "heating up" of a society around an issue through the "saturation" of all available channels of communication. In a "hot" society, all channels of communication and the processes of individual and social change reinforce a message. From the perspective of designing an education and communication programme, this might be called the "saturation" approach to social change.

Example of 'Saturation'

A decade ago, research information about the link between smoking and chronic disease, particularly cancer and heart attack, was communicated to health professionals in a hostile environment where smoking was considered socially "in". But information campaigns by governments and cancer/heart associations put smoking on the public agenda. The result? Conversations about smoking increased within households, doctors' offices and in laboratories. Community organisations began to take action. Schools and the work place joined in.

No-smoking campaigns became a catalyst for change in attitudes and behaviour in health with "smoking" as a unifying symbol. Under the umbrella of "smoking", the rituals and behaviours associated with smoking were individually affected by the saturation process. Therefore other health activities related to smoking also reaped the benefits. Extending the impact of saturation can be applied to other contexts.

Today, a new global image is emerging—an image which represents the environment and unifies people behind its common cause. The symbol of a "Green" earth and the colour "green" are perpetuating an environmental movement, the result of and an inspiration to environmental education and communication efforts everywhere.

"Green" political parties are gaining popular support. All over the world "green" label marketing approaches are influencing consumer behaviour. Just as in the smoking example, acting upon the unifying symbol of "green" through environmental education and communication has the potential to strengthen programmes and further heat up public consciousness. Environmental education and communication provides the opportunity to support policy change, institutional change and behaviour change in highly segmented audiences.

Stage 1: Setting the Public Agenda

Globally, the public is already talking about the environment. Numerous single-issue environmental groups and educational programmes are already in operation. People become ready to talk about, think about and support environmental activities. Membership in existing environmental groups increases, and new programmes and opportunities for popular participation appear.

Stage 2: Engaging Key Institutions

Building alliances and collaboration among institutions creates a network. Lead institutions reach out to other institutions representing social process—education, work, religion and government—and initiate collaborative educational activities. For example, school systems integrate environmental modules within existing curricula and initiate teacher training and youth ecoclubs. Community based action increasingly addresses local issues such as garbage collection and industrial pollutants. Media coverage responds more frequently and positively.

Stage 3: Establishing a New Environmental Order

Governmental and non-governmental institutions become the initiators of environmental education, and participation becomes broader and more diverse. Specific target audiences begin to modify their role with regard to particular environmental problems. Community mobilisation increasingly generates demand for appropriate regulatory change. Expectations for appropriate individual and social behaviour begin to change. Finally, "Green" positions become "in", "non-Green" positions "out".

Applied Research

Experience with development communication in other sectors leads to optimism in reaching new levels of excellence in combining environmental education and communication. Perhaps the most important element in "putting it all together", however, is to maintain commitment to well-tried applied research procedures.

- Investigation of target audience characteristics (including socio-economic, gender and cultural) and attributes (attitudinal and behavioural) in relation to local environmental issues provides insight into an appropriate model of behaviour change and effective educational strategies, messages and materials.
- Limited testing of innovative strategies devised for local situations will uncover refinements needed for broader application.
- Comparison studies between the impact of different educational strategies with similar objectives will provide a basis for future strategic choices.
- Standardised indicators of impact and evaluation studies will provide an assessment of the progress and impact of programmes and, to some extent, the relative power of different components within the programmes.
- Content analyses of mass media over time will provide profiles of societies "heating up" on environmental issues.
- Description of the differences between industrialised country and developing country objectives, programme content and impact will provide a source of new insight about the process of social and individual change.

In addition, applied research can also advance the state of the art for environmental education and communication when properly field tested. There are two major sources for such innovation:

1. the refinement of social change theory at universities and research firms;
2. "creative" concepts with proved efficacy in other sectors such as the "enter-educate" approach (education through entertainment) in the population sector.

This description of the potential and progress of environmental education and communication is, in reality, a call to action. The "heating up" of societies on environmental issues is technically within our reach through environmental education and communication programmes. It is up to us to develop the funding, the research-based strategies—and the communication among professionals about results, both successes and failure—required to make it happen.

12

Government Intervention and Private Enterprise

Poverty reduction is impossible if the economy does not flourish, driven by a dynamic private sector. However, a purely market-led strategy simply increases corporate profits. It does not help a national economy to develop. Japan and the East Asian "tiger states" took a different approach. In these cases, strong governments competently directed private enterprise. Development policy should consider this model.

Cashew nuts are a popular snack with an evening beer but, far more importantly, they are a major economic asset for a number of African countries. Tanzania and Guinea-Biassau each account (or accounted) for 8 per cent of world production. Ivory Coast for six per cent and Mozambique for three per cent. The importance of cashew nuts is even clearer if looked at from the countries perspective. They were Mozambique's second largest export product for a long time-next to sugar. Today, however, most of the factories which processed cashew nuts for export have closed down in Mozambique and Tanzania. This has been caused by the privatisation and liberalisation policy of the World Bank and the International Monetary Fund. What happened?

Mozambique had built up an industry processing cashew nuts for export. In 1994-95, at the insistence of the World Bank, the 18 state owned businesses, with approximately

10,000 employees, were privatised and passed into the hands of local business people. No sooner had this happened, than the World Bank released a study which claimed that the processing industry was so inefficient that the country was losing money. The bank said it would be more profitable to export raw nuts to India: the country's export earnings would increase, as would farmer's incomes. Until then, Mozambique's government had banned the export of unprocessed nuts in order to protect its own industry. The multilateral organisations now made the free export of cashews a strict condition for further loans and the government found itself forced to lift the ban.

As a result, most of the businesses had to cease production (in 2005, only seven of the 18 were still in operation). Nonetheless, farmers did not make any more money than before. Middlemen were pocketing the profit, factory workers were on the streets and export earnings dropped. Whereas Mozambique earned $ 151 million in 1971 from cashew exports, the figure had gone down to only $ 11.5 million by 2005.

In a study carried out subsequently at the personal request of World Bank President James Wolfensohn, then Bank stated that the policy imposed on Mozambique was totally wrong and should be abandoned. It said that the Indian cashew nut industry was only profitable thanks to states subsidies and that, in Mozambique, the value added by processing was a reason to keep the industry alive. It had, however, already been ruined. The latest development was that two transnational corporations (OLAM from Singapore and TechnoServe, a US based organisation) formed a partnership in February 2005 to revive the cashew industry in four African countries (including Mozambique). OLAM is the world's largest processor of cashew nuts and also controls the Indian market and TechnoServe has the latest technology. Multinationals are taking over.

Serving Corporate Interests

Perhaps it was a mere coincidence that OLAM and

TechnoServe appeared on the scene. However, an explanation might also be found in a book which appeared on the New York Times 2004 bestseller list "Confessions of an Economic Hit Man" by John Perkins. The author describes how he travelled all over the world, commisioner by the US government and multinationals, to draw the governments of third world countries into a network of US interests, to make them financially dependent and bring them under political and economic control. Perkins describes cases similar to the one above, and others such as that of the Iranian Prime Minister, Mossadegh, who nationalised the American oil Companies and was thereupon ousted from office. Companies such as Bechtel and Halliburton are named, which recently played disreputable roles in Iraq. These cases are always about restricting the opportunities for autonomous national economic decisions and making the third world countries dependent on the US.

The following case (not one of Perkin's) is another such example. Ghana has some of the world's largest bauxite reserves. After Ghana's independence in 1957, one of President Nkrumah's top goals was to exploit these reserves. Four things were needed: mining the bauxite, an aluminium smelter, sufficient production of electricity and a port. The country funded construction of the port—the colonial government had handed over healthy coffers. The Volta Dam, which allowed cheap electricity to be produced, was financed by an American loan (after Nkrumah had threatened to ask the Soviet Union for funds). An Amerian consortium, Kaiser/Reynolds, built the aluminium smelter VALCO. This left the most important thing: the bauxite mine. But it was made clear to Nkrumah that this could not be financed too. A contract provide that alumina (the intermediate product between bauxite ore and aluminium) should be imported for ten years—from far-off Jamaica. After ten years, this would be reconsidered.

The Volta Dam delivered the first electricity in 1965, aluminium production began in 1966, Nkrumah as ousted in a coup on in 1967. There are still rumours that the US was involved. The bauxite reserves in Kibi, which is barely 100 km from the port of Tema, were never mined and the contract was still in force until recently. Since there was no duty on the alumina imported and the aluminium exported, Ghana never really reaped any benefits from the project. VALCO was sold by Kaiser to Ghana in 2004. The Plant no longer yielded adequate profit with increased cost of electricity. Bauxite mining is now once again under discussion.

The two examples of the cashew nut industry in Mozambique and the aluminium smelter in Ghana clearly show the blessings associated with private enterprise—for internationally active corporations, not for the countries concerned. In both cases, governments were not strong enough to protect the interests of their national economies from the large corporations and other strategic allies. This is one version of how private enterprise development can take place.

Active Governments in East Asia

There is another version which is typical of the East Asian tiger states. It first occurred in Japan and then, following the example, in South Korea and Taiwan, finally in Malaysia and Thailand too. These countries have developed their economies, raised the standard of living for their people and all but eliminated poverty. They did adopt the private, capitalist model for development, but not the market-led-variety. The state kept the leading role for itself. This should not be confused with the state-owned economy found in socialist countries. Here, we are dealing with the model of private enterprise directed by the state.

Japan, an industralised country even before World War II, had to rebuild its economy after 1945. This was done through "administrative guidance" in other words, in close cooperation of government and corporations. The most important state agencies involved were the Ministry of

International Trade and Industry (MITI), the Economic Planning Agency (EPA) and the central bank. Special branches in all government bodies ("mirror units") took care of those industries that planners considered most promising. These were targeted by the State for Support and enjoyed preferential credits, subsidised import of machine tools, upgrading of infrastructure, grants for joint research projects and the protection from excessive competition. The Japanese market was shielded from imports for a considerable time, until its own industry was competitive and able to export. This strategy was so effective that Japan soon became an efficient competitor of the old industralised countries.

Development in the "small tiger states" did not follow the Japanese model in all details, but there were more similarities than differences. State control was more rigorous in South Korea (a development dictatorship") than it was in Japan—but the instruments used were similar. The main players in economic development were the large private conglomerates, or "Chaebol", which are similar to the "Keiretsu" in Japan (a set of companies with interlocking business relationships and shareholdings). Apart from state planning specifications, these conglomerates were closely connected to the state by recruiting civil servants as their senior staff. In Taiwan, there were more state owned industries to start with (they clocked up 50 per cent of all industrial value added in 1952). Even in the 1970s and 1980s, state-owned companies were still being set up in industries with high investment costs (steel, ship building, the automotive industry). Only later were they privatised. But as early as the 1960s, there also was rapid growth in small and medium sized enterprises. Their share of exports amounted to 65 per cent in 1988. In both countries, there was a land reform early on, which set the basis for an equitable distribution of wealth and, at the same time, made available the funds for the industrial development.

A second generation of tiger states, Malaysia, Thailand and Indonesia, followed this model with some variations.

Malaysia's longstanding Prime Minister Mahathir, designing a Look-East Polilcy, explicity deviated from the European-American model. The Pioneer Industries Ordinance of 1958 set the direction and was later replaced by the Investment Incentives Act. The other countries had similar laws.

In all these cases, it was decisive that there was (to varying degrees) a "rational bureaucracy" (as defined by Max Weber) which did not merely look at the country with predators eyes. To be sure, there was and is corruption. However, bureaucrats were always well aware that one must first invest before one can reap benefits. Following the model of MITI and EPA in Japan, state planning agencies were set up, which gave the political specifications for economic development: the Economic Planning Board in Korea, the Council for Economic Planning and Development in Taiwan, the Economic Planning Unit in Malaysia, the National Economic and Social Development Board in Thailand. The intellectual elites of the civil service were gathered this way. They followed external advice only if that served the country. Foreign investment (in principle welcome by all means) was subject to strict conditions.

Oskar Weggel, a Hamburg-based Asia expert, confirms that this policy was good for the people of those countries, saying that, astonishingly, growth did not distort the distribution of incomes but, on the contrary, led to a fair distribution which is almost unique worldwide. In the meantime, as the third generation, Mainland China and Vietnam are following the model. They have not yet reached the same stage of development.

Lessons for Poor Countries

The East Asian countries are the only countries in the world to have reached a level of economic and social development similar to Europe and its derivatives in North America and Australia. Neither real socialism in East Europe nor anarchic capitalism in Lain America led to comparable results. Therefore, the question arises what conclusions can be drawn from the Asian experiences for other poor countries in the world. I believe that government-coordinated private enterprise, rather than market liberalism, is the model which national economies should follow if they are to prosoper.

There can no longer be any doubt that the Washington Consensus has failed. However, its successor, the Post Washington Consensus, only has a vague orientation towards poverty eradication. Nobody has a precise idea what instruments might serve effective implementation. In its justification of a research project called "0perationalising pro-poor growth", the KfW development bank states: "Currently, our knowledge is limited concerning which political measures have to be taken in order to increase the broad-scale impact of economic growth processes." Hopes are mainly directed at an increase in development aid, which could then be used to expand the social sector. There is almost no mention of economic development in the Poverty Reduction Strategy papers, the most important achievement in recent anti-poverty policy. And this while nobody doubts that economic growth is a necessary requirement for poverty reduction.

The creation of an "enabling environment" is still the last word on how to stimulate economic development. However, it has for long been obvious that, on its own, this strategy only leads to cherry-picking by local and foreign investors. They look for individual investment options that are profitable (such as aluminium in Ghana). However, this does not contribute to the development of the national economy, but only serves shareholder interests.

The early development economists in the 1950s and 1960s such as Hirschman, Nurkse and Rosenstein-Rodan, were right after all. Hirsahman expected impulses for development from his concept of "forward and backward linkages", through processinig chains in other words. Rosenstein-Rodan recommended the "big push", simultaneously supporting several industries. The names of these development theorists have wronlgy been forgotten. Paul Krugman, one of the most celebrated economists today, called this approach "high development theory" in 1994 and stated that it "really does make a lot of sense, after all".

If development policy is truly interested in starting the economic development of third world countries in corporation with private partners, then it should endeavour to learn from the East-Asian model in some or at least one of its priority countries. This would require first, support for the creation of a Planning Board. A number of well-trained and motivated planners and economists originating from the country in question should be recalled from wherever they are currently employed (Europe, USA, international organisations) and be paid attractive salaries. Their task would then be to design an economic and social master plan which should amount to more than a mere wish list. Finally, adequate funds would have to be made available to implement the plan among other things, to draw private investors into the country with appropriate tax and other incentives (but not by providing rent-opportunities).

13

Caught in the Debt Trap?

The Foreign Indebtedness of Developing Countries

The question of whether there is a way out of the developing countries' debt trap can only be properly answered if their indebtedness is not viewed as an isolated factor. It should be seen in the context of the total net resource flows into these countries. The following facts must be borne in mind:

1. Net resource flows to developing countries increased from 1994 to 1995 by 11.5 per cent of US $ 231.3 bn. The greatest share was made up of private sector flows, which accounted for 72 per cent ($167.1 bn) of total transfer inputs;
2. Of the private flows, foreign direct investments totalling $ 90.3 bn dominate. Their well above average increase reflects the globalisation of production and growing integration of developing and transformation countries in the world economy. To date, however, this has applied mainly to 12 countries on which about 80 per cent of private inflows is concentrated. These are China, Mexico, Brazil, South Korea, Malaysia, Argentina, Indonesia, Thailand, Russia, India, Turkey and Hungary;
3. Portfolio equity flows to developing countries known for their high sensitivity on earnings and policy have

dropped markedly for the time being to $ 22 bn. This is a not unexpected reaction to:

- the sharp rise in US interest rates since February 1994 and a very positive trend on the American capital market;
- the Mexican Peso crisis which began in December 1994; and
- the more cautious evaluation of the risks of investments in emerging markets, which major institutional investors believe have reached a certain degree of saturation.

4. Official development finance totalled $ 64.2 bn. of which, the World Bank reported, $ 11 bn was allocated to the rescue action for Mexico alone. ODA in 1995 stagnated at $ 47 bn. Its proportion of the OECD donor countries' GDPs was 0.29 per cent, the lowest since the beginning of the 1970s. The main reasons for this downturn were the industrial nations' well-known public budget problems and the fact that more creditworthy development and transformation countries are increasingly procuring their finance on private capital markets. Understandably, large sums were made available, mainly by Germany, to Eastern Europe and the successor states to the former Soviet Union. From strictly developmental viewpoints, it is disquieting that ever fewer ODA funds are available for longer-term development projects due to their disbursement for short-term emergency and crisis assistance.

The Washington Decisions

The recent annual conference of G7 finance ministers and central bank chiefs took the following decisions:

1. About 20 highly indebted poor countries (HIPCs) were to be reviewed to establish whether in endeavouring to solve their debt problems they could expect greater support from the international donor community than

previously. There was a justified fear that without enhanced assistance, and continuing to employ only the instruments used to date, these countries would not even achieve an acceptable level of indebtedness within the next 5-10 years;

2. *Time horizon:* in two three-year stages, a comprehensive review of the indebtedness and adjustment measures the affected countries could cope with would be undertaken. This would include observing the impacts of employing the customary instruments of debt relief. If the results were unsatisfactory, the new measures decided in Washington, which were expected to achieve a positive breakthrough, would be applied as well after three to six years; In detail, these are:
   - *Paris Club* (official creditors): rescheduling of bilateral debts, with case-to-case remission of up to 80 per cent compared with a current ceiling of 67 per cent;
   - Comparable relief conditions through non-Paris Club and private creditors (London Club);
   - *IMF:* grants from the Enhanced Structural Adjustment Facility (ESAF) or long-term ESAF loans. The recipient countries use these sums for debt servicing; and
   - redemption of multilateral debts from a future HIPC trust fund to be administered by the IDA. Setting up the fund will formally ensure that it is not a matter of debt remission.

3. *Financing:* provisional estimates put the cost of the HIPC initiative at around $ 6 bn. This is to be funded by the Paris Club members, third-party creditors and international finance institutions. Two factors of the total costs are uncertain;

   These are the number of countries which in the end will be given access to the funds, and the realism of the estimates of export income upon which the country analyses are based.

4. *Assessment:* all in all, the HIPC initiative is a fresh attempt to substantially relieve these countries of their debt problems, and support their economic reform programmes and measures to alleviate poverty. The World Bank and IMF were directed to begin implementing the debt initiative without delay and report back to the conference of the supervisory bodies in the spring of this year. Leading donor countries were able to agree to the initiative because:

   - financial integrity, particularly the preferential creditor status of the World Bank, the IMF and the regional development banks, was not in question;
   - The debtor countries were not relieved of their basic responsibility for comprehensive and sustainable adjustment policies; and finally
   - The usual case-to-case procedure, taking decisions from country to country, was retained.

Global Impacts

To complete the "indebtedness picture", two other important problem areas must be pointed out. The problems and risks arising from the HIPCs' indebtedness affect first and foremost the national and, at worst, the regional level of the countries concerned. A serious endangering of the global finance and currency system must not be allowed to emanate from them. However, and this is the first problem, it can be much graver in the case of advanced developing countries, as Mexico showed in 1995. The risks which arise for the money and capital markets from liberalisation of short-term movements of capital in a number of threshold countries with large issue volumes are considerable. Strictly speaking, the capital market securities acquired in these markets by nationals and foreigners are only partly foreign debts.

However, because they can be sold at any time and their convertibility and transferability is guaranteed, they can present similarly high risks for the solvency of the country concerned as "traditional" foreign debts. Additionally, the fact that "maturity" here depends not on contractually agreed terms, but on fragile investor confidence, enhances, the risks.

The large sums deployed in the Mexico rescue action organised by the USA and IMF show that endangerment of the international finance system was on hand. Above all, what the financial world aptly labelled the "Tequila effect"—a chain reaction of investors making a mass flight out of other threshold countries such as Brazil, Argentina and the Philippines, which threatened to spread—called for comprehensive confidence-building measures.

Not least, this experience was the basis for the agreement by the G7 ministers and central bankers in Washington on initial steps of a new IMF crisis financing mechanisms. Thus, the General Agreement on Credits was doubled to Special Drawing Rights of $ 34 bn.

Conclusion

The conclusion that must be drawn from this development are:

- to strengthen the IMF's role as a catalyst and improve its surveillance function;
- to bring the G7 group in their own interest to put in place stable economic general conditions, above all harmonised control of the interest rates of the key currencies; and
- to support the threshold countries in creating credible political conditions, especially by stabilising their economic, financial and currency policies in order to give no cause for sudden crises of confidence.

❋ ❋ ❋

14

Aid Effectiveness as a Multi-level Process

Parallel to the widespread decrease of aid resources provided by donor countries to developing countries in recent years, debate and research on how to make aid more effective has become a major concern. Usually, it is suggested that decades of development assistance have at best produced marginal results in terms of improving development levels in the South. Little mention is made of donor's policy shortcomings and the negative impact of these on efforts aimed at reforming and redefining development cooperation in order to enhance aid effectiveness. The policy parameters and operating frameworks of existing aid policies continue to inhibit higher degrees of aid effectiveness. In many donor countries, opinion polls indicate waning public support for development aid.

Increasingly, the moral case for aid is called into question and deeper world market integration tends to be seen as the panacea to continued economic decline and social destabilisation in the South. Against this background, cooperation between donor and recipient actors is faced with a duel uphill struggle. First, fewer resources can be mobilised to meet growing developmental needs. On the other hand, to organise and manage development policies and programmes in a result-oriented manner, grows more difficult. The threat of further aid cuts and of further drops of public support for providing aid become ever more real. A closer look at the organisational complexities and political constraints under which development cooperation is expected to perform effectively may help to improve current aid management approaches.

Towards Conceptual Clarity

At first sight, catchy definitions of what constitutes effective aid might appear attractive to use, in particular with regard to economic indicators. The term "aid effectiveness" is easily used in the same vein as "efficiency", "significance" or "impact" of aid. At times, obsession to measure and demonstrate the results of aid supported development processes can be observed among policy-makers and administrators on the donor side. Still the understanding of aid and its effectiveness as being part and parcel of a cooperation relationship between donor and recipient side parties, is scarcely embedded in practice. To determine how to make aid more effective requires more than a quick impact analysis of an individual and perhaps even isolated development project. Consequently, defining the concept of aid effectiveness needs to take into account at what levels cooperation is focused on. To strive for sustainable and effective modes of development cooperation will entail the need to combine recipient ownership of the development process with donor accountability concerns.

Performance expectations cannot be exclusively placed on the recipient while donor interests, their aid management systems and procedures remain unchanged.

An extended and more analytical, process-oriented definition should take into account four main aspects of aid effectiveness:

(a) Effective aid must relate to the building and/or strengthening of in-country aid management capacity;

(b) To maximise the degree of aid effectiveness, local ownership of the aid process is essential: from setting

of priorities through policy formulation and implementation on to the evaluation stages of the process;

(c) Increasing recipient side capabilities to take charge of aid relationship, will need to be combined with arrangements to meet legitimate donor accountability concerns;

(d) Aid effectiveness is a two-faceted objective: its realisation is equally dependent on increased transparency of donor motives and on dropping of non-developmental, political and economic aid objectiveness of donors.

In addition a broader range of stakeholders in the aid relationship needs to be actively involved: extending beyond accountable government and implementing agencies, to include democratic institutions and organisations of civil society and of the private sector.

Applying any definition of aid effectiveness without disaggregating macro-economic data and taking into account country specificity will only lead to unhelpful generalisations about aid and its effectiveness. It would seem more appropriate to adopt working definitions against which to assess effectiveness of aid resources at a country-specific level. On such a basis one could expect to arrive at more reliable indicators of how well aid resources contribute to improving developmental standards and meeting existing needs.

From Definition to Success—Key Requirements

Having reached agreement between the recipient and donor on what should constitute effectiveness of aid is only a starting point. Embarking on democratic, peaceful and participatory patterns of economic and social development must follow: to arrive at significant and lasting improvement in many of the least developed countries will be a long-term process. This being said, it is crucial to design and implements such forms of development cooperation which involve a wide range of recipient side actors, not only from the government side but also from civil society at large. Seen as a process of increasing inclusion of intended beneficiaries of aid, the commitment to decentralise as well as entrust aid and its management grows in importance.

To fully capture Third World development realities, policy frameworks inspired by neoliberalist-type of development concepts and theories are grossly inadequate. The views and positions on aid articulated in the World Bank and the IMF, or in many if not most bilateral aid administrations in OECD countries, represent only one side of today's international cooperation, namely the donor side. The major weakness to point out with respect to this locus of debate, is a profound under representation if not even a total absence of recipient experiences and perceptions on aid in general and on its effectiveness in particular. There should be little doubt that ignoring to not actively identifying and involving such perceptions, leads to strongly donor driven aid.

To circumvent recipient side insights and views on strengths and weaknesses of aid strategies and mechanisms, will result in limited local commitment and sense of ownership over the aid process. Mutual decision-making between donors and recipients remains a rare policy approach. Aid procedures that are based on local management and less control-oriented donor roles in the aid process are still exceptions in development cooperation.

Structurally, in terms of the policy environment within which development aid is expected to function, the overriding policy framework is general based on structural adjustment policies (SAP). But the underlying conclusion made by proponents of SAPs that these policies induce aid effectiveness, has yet to be proven valid. It must suffice at this point to emphasize that there is no *a priori* relationship between world market integration under structural adjustment and sustainable development in poor countries.

Aid to these countries which is solely intended to reinforce fundamentally uneven and unequal patterns of world market integration should be scrutinised critically.

Some central issues need to be addressed in the course of improving aid and its effectiveness:

- institutional dimensions of aid relationships require strong policy-attention, both on the donor and the recipient side;
- capacities to effectively identify and formulate aid priorities need to be strengthened in recipient countries;
- local capacities to sustain reform efforts must be reinforced.

Levels of Intervention

If the design of aid and the terms upon which it is provided to a developing country are largely determined by the donor, the aid relationship can be characterised as essentially hierarchical. Recipient side views will rarely surface, as they are either not identified, or not well formulated. Possibilities of a recipient-led development strategies can be limited. Unless scope is provided to the recipient side actors to assume responsibilities, aid effectiveness is likely to remain low or fluctuating, and the sustainability of donor aid efforts will remain doubtful.

National planning processes and courses of national development in recipient countries should be seen as most effective where they are led under local responsibility and control. To arrive at this ideal situation, gaps need to be reduced and closed at the various intervention levels.

Donor aid resources provide valuable support for this process. Their effectiveness in meeting long-term objective of aid will need to be assessed on the basis of how well they perform at the different levels. Individual donors will expectedly perform differently at the various levels. What will prove to be the ultimate test for effectiveness is how well the donor aid performance accomplishes the broader objectives of development cooperation and how well it includes sustainable results.

In the analytical frameworks outlined here, development cooperation would seem to be confronted with the effectiveness gaps at the:

- *Structural Level:* International trade and investment patterns, debt problems and world market integration process appear as long-term constraining factors upon aid and its effectiveness;
- *Policy Level:* Dialogue and partnership in development cooperation are instrumental factors in recluding planning and co-ordination gaps with regard to policy analysis and formulation;
- *The Institutional Level* is where pertinent capacity gaps exist: capacity development efforts of donors and technical assistance measures play an important role in addressing weaknesses in aid effectiveness within a country's institutional setting;
- Finally, at the *level of aid projects* (programmes), it is generally the lack of sustainability of aid interventions which causes development activities to falter once donor support decreases or stops. In addition to technical cooperation, financial and material inputs serve to maintain project momentum and goal realisation. The issue of how to develop local capacity sufficiently in order for indigenous organisations to continue project activities initially supported by donor aid, remains the most important issue to address at this level.

Fostering Aid Effectiveness

Donor and recipient development efforts are too often isolated from one another, or poorly coordinated. They fail to address managerial and implementation bottlenecks. Cross-sectorial linkages, as well as interdisciplinary approaches to aid problems are only slowly gaining ground. It is increasingly obvious, that decisions on aid issues are subjected to concerns outside of the responsible ministry: finance ministers, and unfortunately even defence ministers have a strong say in how much aid is to be provided, where it is to be concentrated and under what terms to be utilised. Inside of recipient countries, large portions of national budgets are allocated to non-development priorities with little or no impact on alleviating urgent poverty problems.

Development cooperation may make the biggest impact and be executed most effectively where donors and recipients agree upon multi-level aid strategies. To give an example, building a road to a remote rural area may well be done in an effective project manner. It is equally important to have a functioning transport authority in place to ensure maintenance of the roads. If this authority operates within a nationally defined infrastructure policy, best in accord with national trade and investment priorities, then the effectiveness of the project-level road building programme has a good chance of being high.

Institutional changes to set the stage for a profound reform process in development cooperation are needed. Reprioritising national budgets to reflect identified in country development needs may be one step. Setting up policy evaluation and formulation units can be complimentary measures. Deregulating markets and investment rules may serve to please donors, but dumping of cheap products which strangle local production efforts may easily result. Regional cooperation, including intensified South-South cooperation can provide some counterbalance. There are only a few areas where changes in the current system of development cooperation can occur, with a view to better manage the complexities of aid and the social, cultural, economic and political backgrounds against which they take place. The will and commitment to take policy action in both donor and recipient countries, through the broadest range of stakeholders and institutions as possible, will be the test for genuine efforts at improving development relations between North and South and organising cooperation effectively.

❄ ❄ ❄

15

Tourism and the Environment

The relationship between tourism and the environment is obvious, and is largely established through what is sometimes called "environment quality". This quality is perceived in different ways according to the human population and the circumstances presiding tourist activities at any given moment. Any analysis of the relationship between tourism and the environment that we can include under human ecology therefore comprises aspects of the natural sciences as well as the social sciences.

Tourist activity is promoted, conditioned and influenced by the environmental circumstances of each region and can be affected by modifications or changes in those circumstances. Although a lot of emphasis has been placed on the negative impact or modifications in "environment quality" attributed to tourism, it is also accepted that it can be a very important factor in the preservation and defence of ecological values threatened by more destructive alternatives for the use of territory. Very often, tourism can be the most suitable and most satisfactory way of using a region's renewable natural resources. Nevertheless, their management and use need to be properly regulated so as to guarantee their renewability and persistence.

There is room in this complex field of relations to study, rationalise and optimise an activity as important as tourism, from the point of view of its insertion in the ecological systems with which it interacts. However, there are relatively few efficient studies on issues of real importance. It is startling to observe that places with tourist potential undertake little or no research in this field.

One possible cause is the difficulty in identifying the real problematic in tourism/environment relations, which is essentially interdisciplinary and involves the integration of traditionally separate areas of knowledge. Although work is undertaken from time to time on environmental psychology, the sociology of tourism, behaviour in relation to the environment, etc., they are very rarely combined with works on the environment, forestry and agricultural policies, soil use, contamination, bio-diversity, evaluation of environmental impact, nature conservation, etc., in search for a more integrated management of tourist resources.

Responsible Tourism

Tourism runs the risk of going the way of other phenomena, which first of all experience rapid growth and then suffer a spectacular collapse, what in Economics is often called "boom and bust",

The causes are familiar: a certain dose of greed, often based on a lack of mid-or long-term planning, property speculation, little consideration for local populations—in both economic and social aspects—and, in general, a lack of awareness as regards environmental aspects—contamination, water use, energy, etc., — on the part of tour operators, hoteliers and other agents involved in tourism in its different forms, including the tourists themselves. The problem is particularly evident in eco-tourism, based on the wonders of the natural world: landscapes, flora and fauna. Many experts fear for the future of this type of tourism, which has grown spectacularly in the last few years. Landscapes deteriorate, the fauna decreases, the designers and administrators of tourist developments fail to respect the most elementary principles for adapting architecture to its surroundings, or else there is little effort to recycle, economise or educate with a few honourable exceptions, tourist planning is careless and irresponsible.

And yet a responsible approach would be in the tour operators' own interests, as it would make the tourist industry sustainable, with positive influences on biological, economic and social aspects.

Eco-tourism, for example, has shown that when properly conceived it can become a powerful instrument for the preservation of nature, with very favourable repercussions for local populations and for educational programmes, while offering hundreds of millions of eco-tourists a wide range of spiritual and physical satisfactions. At the same time, the host countries can take pride in what they have to offer their citizens and the rest of the world.

The preventive and corrective measures are known to us, what is needed is a sense of responsibility and farsightedness on the part both of the authorities and of the industry. We need regulations and controls, so as to put the people who do the damage out of circulation and reward those at the forefront of sustainability.

Sustainable Tourism

After several decades of rapid quantitative growth, tourism is going through a period of profound transformation. Tourists, the consumers in this industry, but also the public, have started to demand a change in the conditions of production and use of tourist services, putting an end to the uncontrolled expansion of mass tourism.

This is the ultimate reason, apart from ethical and aesthetic consideration, why tourist activity as a whole, in the private sector as well as in the public and voluntary (NGO) sector, has begun to seriously analyse the implication of tourism in terms of socio-cultural and environmental impacts, and to consider the need to draw up and implement environment friendly tourist policies.

Indeed, while not denying the viability and the utility of alternative approaches of an external and coercive nature, it is obvious that the decision-makers in the sector react better to positive stimuli. The realisation that their clients prefer well-conserved areas and non-aggressive tourist practices and that they are prepared to pay more for this makes it easier to adopt strategies of sustainability in the tourist industry in a sincere alliance with conservation movements.

All this points to the validity of Overall Quality Management as a viable method in sustainable tourist activities. The overall quality approach renders the management of products and especially of tourist areas extremely sensitive to the preferences and expectations of consumers. The private public profitability of a tourist destination will depend on client's satisfaction, since these will return more often and for longer and will pass on a positive image of their holiday experiences. In so far as these preferences and expectations include the demand for unspoilt settings, consumer satisfaction, and therefore the profitability of a tourist spot, will call for the development of strategies for sustainable development.

One can believe this is a productive approach for sustainability in the tourist business and one that makes for professional attitudes that fit in with the economic targets of businesses and other organisations. There is only one prior requirement: continued education and training of everyone involved in tourism, from consumers to those responsible for tourist policies. The demand for quality, and even more so for environmental quality, is a call to people's awareness, to their understanding of the environmental and cultural implication of any activity and their ability to express themselves and to organise to choose the most clear-sighted line of action.

Tourism in the Modern Age

What will the tourist trade of the year 2000 be like? Who will be the tourists of the coming millennium? These are the questions which, faced with the extraordinary boom in tourism, expert, tour operators and politicians have repeatedly posed over the last fifteen years. These questions arise either because of the financial profits the tourist industry involves, or from the demands of consumers who show new awarenesses, habits and lifestyles. In the eighties, mass tourism gradually changed and people began to talk of "tourisms". Expressions such as cultural tourism, sports tourism, religious tourism, adventure tourism or eco-tourism have become part of everyday language. In the past the dominant practices was to take one long holiday in a single destination. Today, people tend to distribute their holidays over different destinations and different times of the year.

From a socio-historical point of view, three types of tourist industry can be differentiated. In the case of the industrial tourist, for whom work is the center of existence, the motivations for travelling can be summed up as rest and freedom from responsibilities. This type is gradually decreasing in number. The hedonistic tourist belongs to the generation that discovered entertainment and consumerism. They like to go on holiday to experiment, to explore the unknown, enjoy themselves meet other people and relax in unspoilt natural surroundings. These are the majority today and will continue to be so. Finally, the modern age tourist, someone who tends to reduce the polarity between work and play: not just work, but just not fun, either. Their reasons for travelling include broadening their personal horizons and getting back to simple things and nature, with a touch of creativity in the planning of their journey. These are gradually growing in number and in future will form an important segment of demand.

One characteristic in the expectations of the modern age tourist is the capacity to make a critical appraisal of the offer and to influence it. Producers should be more attentive and sensitive to the new demands and be flexible enough to cater for the tourist in search of higher quality. In the third millennium in fact, the concept of quality will have to take environmental aspects more into account. Recent forms of tourism point to a renewed interest in nature and a wish for quality tourism. So much so, that some tourist spots are reorganising their own offer in keeping with these trends. Quality is the result of a complex strategy which is organised day by day. The consumers, whose environmental awareness is constantly growing, will expect to identify, verify and be able to differentiate ecologically correct products from the imitations now invading the market.

The present millennium is coming to an end and is leaving Western countries with a high level of welfare and a large tourist demand to satisfy. Nevertheless, serious environmental problems also plague areas that receive a high influx of tourists. Tourists, tour operators, local authorities and the general public are therefore called on to find new forms of co-existence and the right solutions for themselves and for the survival of the planet.

16

Fresh Water and the Environment

It is widely recognised that water is going to be one of the major issues confronting humanity at the turn of the century and beyond. We are facing a crisis as regards the quantity and quality of water supply, but we have yet to experience full social and political impact of that crisis. The escalation in the population and the quest for continued development is leading to conflicting pressures on water resources. Such resources are the ultimate recipient of pollution from various socio-economic activities associated with urbanisation, agriculture, mining and clearing of native vegetation. Pollution originating from human waste, especially where appropriate sanitation facilities are not available, or are located too close to water supply sources affects both surface water and ground water.

This makes water supply and health perhaps the most important issue for the large proportion of the global population. Paradoxically, the demands for "sustainable management" and increasing global population require more potable water from a declining available potable water base.

It is universally accepted that proper water administration is a critical component of sustainable development—that is, development that meets the needs of both present and future generations. Indeed, water is an essential factor in a large number of productive activities, of which one of the most important is the production of food by irrigation. This activity, accounts for two thirds of the water resources used by humanity. A supply of drinking water and sanitation in urban centres are crucial for preserving human health.

For some decades it has been known that the misuse of water resources is responsible for many important environment problems. For example, in many industrialised cities both surface water and ground water are seriously contaminated. This deterioration is a consequence of a range of human activities, sometimes in isolation, others over a large area or a long period of time. Among examples of the latter is modern agriculture, whether it uses irrigation or not, as a result of the intensive use made of mineral fertilizers and pesticides.

Water Shortage: Exaggeration, Reality or Bad Management?

Some of these problems have made news and have created the impression the water shortage will be one of humanity's big problems in the coming decades. Sometimes this feeling is due to genuinely manipulative publicity campaigns to justify the setting in motion of hydraulic megaprojects which basically benefit a few large construction companies. The truth is that except for a handful of very specific cases, no problems of water shortage are to be found almost anywhere. On the other hand, cases of bad water management are not rare at all.

Basic Principles for Good Water Management

Good management of water resources—and of almost all other natural resources—must be based on the principles of solidarity, "subsidiarity" and participation. The physical reality requires that these resources be considered a common heritage of humanity both now and in the future. By "subsidiarity" we mean that water management should be as decentralised as possible: what one person or any minor social group can do should not be done by a higher authority. For example, what local government can do should not be done a regional, state or central government. Participation consists in water users playing as large a part as possible in decisions affecting water, in keeping with each state's or country's social and cultural structure. Obviously this participation calls for a certain cultural and technical knowledge—a hydrological education—on the part of those users.

The need for participation by users is even greater in the exploitation of groundwater. In this case, users tend to extract water independently of one another. They often fail to realize, until there is a serious economic or environmental impact, that their pumping affects other people who rely on the same water supply as has happened.

Water shortage is rarely a serious problem: in fact, in some cases the problem is exaggerated to justify the construction of large works using taxpayer's money. On the other hand, the contamination of surface and groundwater tends to be a problem which rarely receives adequate treatment. Successful water management should be based on three basic principles: solidarity, subsidiarity and participation. The specific way in which these principles are applied will vary from one state or country to another, but the effectiveness of water management will depend in large measure on the hydrological education of the general public.

The universal way of obtaining freshwater is from rain. River systems are the results of the excess water that falls on dry land in the form of rain. On the one hand, rainwater penetrates the permeable soils, saturates them and accumulates to form groundwater reservoirs, or aquifers, which can come to the surface in the form of springs. On the other hand, the water is absorbed by vegetation, which uses it for pumping minerals and then evaporates it by transpiration. Some rainwater is lost because it evaporates immediately on falling on impermeable surfaces like the asphalt of roads and cities. Running water courses finally flow over saturated soils, shaping the complex systems of the watersheds or river basins.

Since each basin's natural system has developed gradually and has grown up according to the yearly distribution and fluctuations of rainfall, we have to appreciate that any large-scale project for redistributing water by means of pipes, as if it were gas or electricity, is a journey into the unknown. This is because it destroys the results of the work of shaping the climate, however transitory it might be.

Variable Volumes

All water supplies are of variable volume. Both the discharge of rivers and the level of lakes and aquifers depend on rainfall. As these resources are components of a larger system, the river basin, a reasonable policy would be to manage water resources according to the characteristics of each basin. This would require, first of all, a proper understanding of the system so as to adapt use and consumption to the existing supply. Conserving river systems as much as possible in their natural state is the best guarantee for the preservation of the landscape and of a constant supply. Groundwater reservoirs aren't canals, but are more like lakes, so that pollution leads to the build-up of a debt which is paid in years to come.

Consumption

Water consumption has increased in recent years as a result of not only population growth but also an increase in living standards. In the rural areas the introduction of new farming methods, the spread of irrigation and the excessive use of fertilizers and pesticides causes very high consumption—it is estimated that more than 2/3 of water consumption is used in irrigating. Agricultural pollution also endangers both surface water and aquifers, which receive water full of chemical products. Many cases of eutrophication, the enrichment of water by nutrients that accelerate the growth of algae, derive from the run-off of fertilizers. The practice of intensive stock-raising on farms with large numbers of animals also brings about these problems of over consumption and pollution. Cleaning the stockyards requires large amounts of water which is then released into the environment with high concentrations of nitrogen.

As for industries, they have in the past taken little care over water consumption and dumping, and in many areas the need for proper attention comes as something new. The best thing would be to make industry take its water at a point down-river from where it returns it or, better still, generalise the use of closed circuit systems based on the constant recycling and reusing of the same water.

As regards human consumption, the general attitude to cleanliness is based on diluting pollutants. One example is the success of the use of the Water Closet which involves diluting a few decilitre of urine in 10 or more litres of drinking water: quite a record in wastefulness.

Another aspect to be considered is the different quality of the water that falls on well formed soils from the water that falls on roads, cities, airports, suburbs and built-up areas and whose composition is less stable and "worse" than that resulting from a more uniform interaction with mature soils. Remember that streets, roofs, communication routes, airports and built-up areas already cover a high proportion of the earth's land area and are still on the increase.

Purification techniques should be based especially on the natural processes that include biological activity. Otherwise—for example, if physico-chemical methods are used—there can be side-effects such as an excess of mud or sediments. The strategy to follow is to optimize operations in our use of water according to the discharge and to the distribution of contamination. A system in the form of a conduit or channel, such as a river, can respond relatively quickly. On the other hand, lakes and dams can only do so up to a point, because they show more inertia and irreversibility and take longer to clean.

Large lakes, not to mention the sea, might seem a good place to dump contaminating refuse, but they can't then be cleaned. This is the price we pass on the future generations: a comfortable attitude, but an unacceptable one.

17

Population Growth and Fresh Water

Wherever population is growing, the supply of fresh water per person is declining. As a result of population growth, the mount of water available per person from the hydrological cycle will fall by 74 per cent between 1950 and 2050. Stated otherwise, there will be only one fourth as much fresh water per person in 2050 as there was in 1950. With water availability per person projected to decline dramatically in many countries already facing shortages, the full social effects of future water scarcity are difficult even to imagine. Indeed spreading water scarcity may be the most underrated resource issue in the world today.

Evidence of water stress can be seen as rivers are drained dry and as water tables fall. The Colorado River in the south-western United States now rarely reaches the sea. The Yellow River, the northernmost of China's two major rivers, has run dry for a part each year since 1985, with the dry period becoming progressively longer. In 1997, it failed to make it to the sea for 226 days. The Nile, the largest river in the Middle East, has little water left when it reaches the sea.

Water tables are now falling on every continent, including in major food-producing regions. Among those where aquifers are being depleted are the U.S. southern Great

Plains the North China Plain, which produces nearly 40 per cent of China's grain; and most of the India. Wherever water tables are falling today, there will be water supply cutbacks tomorrow, as aquifers are eventually depleted.

Some 70 per cent of the water pumped from underground or diverted from rivers is used for irrigation, 20 per cent is used for industrial purposes, and 10 per cent is for residential use. Water use patterns vary widely by region. In Europe, for example, where agriculture is largely rainfed, water withdrawals are dominated by industrial use. In Asia, in contrast, irrigation accounts for 85 per cent of all water use.

As countries press against the limits of their water supplies, the competition among sectors itensifies The economics of water use does not favour agriculture. One thousand tons of water can be used to produce one ton of wheat worth $200 of to expand industrial output by $14,000. This ratio of 70 to 1 explains why industry almost always wins in the competition with agriculture for water.

As the growing demand of water collides with the limits of supply, countries typically satisfy rising urban and residential demands by diverting water from irrigation. They then import grain to offset the loss of irrigation water. Since it takes at least 1,000 tons of water to produce a ton of grain, importing grain becomes the most efficient way to import water. North Africa and the Middle East—a region where population growth is rapid and every country faces water shortages—has become the world's fastest growing grain import market during the 1990s. In 1997, the water required to produce the grain and other foodstuffs imported into the region was roughly equal to the annual flow of the Nile River.

In both China and India, the two countries that together dominate world irrigated agriculture, substantial cutbacks in irrigation water supplies lie ahead. The combination of the effects of aquifer depletion in key countries such as these and the growing diversion of irrigation water to non-farm uses in many countries makes it unlikely that there will be much, if any, increase in total irrigated area over the long term. Already the irrigated area per person has been slowly declining since 1978, falling from a historical high of 0.047 hectares per person to 0.045 hectares in 1996—a drop of 4 per cent. If the total irrigated area remains at roughly 263 million hectares until 2050, this key figure will fall to 0.028 hectares per person in 2050—declining by an additional 38 per cent. Such a shrinkage will pose a formidable challenge to the world's farmers.

About a billion people will be living in countries facing absolute water scarcity by 2025. These nations do not have enough water to maintain 1990 levels of food production per person from irrigated area, even with high irrigation efficiency, and to meet the needs for domestic, industrial, and environmental purposes as well. They will have to reduce water use in agriculture in order to satisfy residential and industrial water needs. The resulting decline in domestic food production will force them to import more food, assuming it is available. Although detailed water projections by sector for each country are not available for 2050, the number of water-deprived people will be far greater than in 2025 if the world continues on the U.N. medium population trajectory. The bottom line is that if we are facing a future of water scarcity, then we are also facing future of food scarcity.

❋ ❋ ❋

18

Employment and Promoting Ecology

How a Service Culture Could Put People Back to Work

We are facing two big and urgent social problems: employment and ecology. Both the unemployment of millions of people and the progressive destruction of the ecosphere are alarming. But they are linked with each other. The 'greening' of industrial products, processes and services could provide many more jobs.

Unemployment has many causes, including:

- Sluggish markets;
- Stagnating or declining purchasing power;
- Growing uncertainty about the future at all levels;
- lack of will and/or ability to innovate.

But joblessness is by far due mostly to the high efficiency of industrial machinery, which produces ever more, ever faster, with ever fewer workers.

Waste of Resources

The extremely high productive use of human labour and the extremely low productive use of resources are manifested by gigantic mountains of waste. Already today, the junked cars on scrap heaps alone would form a line that would reach to the moon. The scene is the same with discarded electrical and electronic appliances. Every year, millions of tons of ovens, washing machines, refrigerators, dishwashers, TV sets, entertainment electronics equipment and small appliances are being wasted.

If we throw away all these things after a relatively short time we are not only being wasteful and irresponsible with resources, but equally so with people's work. For with the products and materials we discard, we also dispose of the human labour they contain. It is imperative that we radically reduce the enormous turnovers of material and energy. In other words, the productivity of raw materials and energy must be markedly increased. Specifically, that means we must draw as many services as possible from one kilogram of material or 1 kWh of energy. Reducing the enormous flows of materials into the industrial system, as well as developing cycles of materials and responsibility (the manufacturer taken back and repairing and/or remanufacturing used products and materials) and the main pillars of a sustainable development that can cope with the future.

The industrialised nations must cut their consumption of raw materials by a factor of about 10 by 2050; if they are to be able to handle the challenges of the future. To achieve that reduction, innovation efforts must be directed at increasing resource productivity and/or ecological efficiency. In particular, strategies to extend the useful life of goods and intensify their use could result in reducing both the speed and volume of the flows of resources to industry.

Increasing Resource Productivity

In dealing with nature, we and industry are facing radical change. This is the transition from environmental protection (preservation of nature and health) to greater resource productivity (which at the same time means greater competitiveness). As a rule, environmental protection costs money, while higher resource productivity usually cuts manufacturing costs and/or increases a company's profitability. If the company can sell the same utility or benefits while using fewer resources, it saves two-fold: in buying raw materials and on waste disposal. Thereby the rule is that goods and components cycles are more profitable than resources cycles, and that the company which is first in the market gains an additional competitive advantage in terms of a lead in knowledge and image. If a service, or benefits in the form of services, can be sold instead of products, the decoupling of company success and materials flows is even greater.

Impacts on Employment

The two social problem areas of work and ecology have to date been perceived and treated separately in politics, in industry and in our own minds. And, I believe, with little result. The link between the two must be established.

The strategies to boost resource productivity would have considerable impacts on the change in industrial structures, on handling existing product inventories, and on employment. In particular, the strategies would lead to a switch of focal point from a raw materials-intensive and use-value-related service economy. This is where another view of profitability comes in. Business management would no longer focus on value added, but on maintenance of value over longer periods based on the intrinsic value of a product. Expressed as a question, the value factor, which would move to the centre of business thinking and dealing, means: how can the utilisation value be improved and sold? How can products be made with as few raw materials and as little energy as possible and create a high benefit as pollutant-free as possible for as long as possible during their entire life-cycle?

With regard to employment, the production of long-life goods would appear at first sight to lead to a reduction in the need for work. In fact, however, the strategies to increase resources productivity have positive net employment impacts. The reason is that saving resources is based in principle on substituting energy by work, rather than the reverse as has been customary to date.

If the useful life of products is extended, that will not only preserve most of the materials and energy they contain as well as the work invested in them. The products will also require a considerable amount of mostly skilled work input. Reconditioning products is as a rule more labour-intensive than manufacturing them. So large-scale reconditioning and repair work increase the number of skilled jobs and at the same time reduces the inflows of materials and energy.

Comparing a car with a life-cycle of 20 years with two others that each have useful lives of 10 years gives a good example. The first car causes an increase in employment per life-year of about 50 per cent in terms of total work input in manufacture, service, repairs and reconditioning while at the same time reducing the energy consumption by half.

Regionalisation of Industry

Extending product service life would also mean replacing energy and/or capital by skilled work, helping to save money to boot. But not only rising costs of disposal, materials and energy would reduce consumption. Increasing transport costs would also mean that carrying all kinds of freight halfway around the world would make less and less business sense. That would result in ever more products and materials being circulated, reconditioned, and recycled or reduced on a regional basis. In turn, that would create regional jobs, and be more profitable as well as more promotive of technology—not only from ecological aspects.

In addition, a way of doing business which encompassed material and responsibility cycles would no longer differentiate between manufacturing and reconditioning, or between marketing and remarketing. The structure of such an economy would be predominantly decentralised and regionalised so that it could adapt itself to the new cycles. It also would benefit from the greater efficiency of the new working practices.

True, jobs would be lost in the sectors of central production, and raw materials extraction and processing. But at the same time, more and higher-skilled jobs would emerge. These would not only be better qualified jobs, but also decentralised because reconditioning, repairs and maintenance must be done near the customer. And that, in turn, would also reduce goods traffic.

In addition, skilled workers would be needed because in many cases of small production runs it makes sense and is also more economical to hire such people. They can work faster and more flexibly—and mostly cheaper—than fully-automated production lines.

There also would be a growing need for maintenance, repairs and reconditioning. More and more people would be wanted for reconditioning, that is, the remanufacturing of old products. As reconditioning involves far more craft work than highly rationalised new production, there would be a positive impact on the labour market if there were more of the former and correspondingly less of the latter.

From Production to Services

Switching to long-life products and changing from selling products to selling use-values would strengthen the current trend of jobs shifting from industrial production to the service sector. For example, if the service of individual transport were to be sold instead of the product car, the company with the competitive advantage would be the one that had a service centre in every town and village, with appropriately staffed workshops and sales or rental facilities.

Enduring change towards a knowledge-intensive and use-value-related service economy would not only mean that more people would be needed to fill jobs. It would offer more opportunities for part-time work, as well as possibilities of employment for older people and the handicapped. People who earlier could not keep up with the pace of working life would be more inclined to return to it. Another impact would be that many companies would reduce their dependence on the world market. They would no longer switch certain tasks abroad, but assign them to their part-time employees, helping them to meet their commitments as self-employed entrepreneurs.

The latter would be accommodated by an ecology-driven fiscal reform which would make massive cuts or changes in subsidies and raise the cost of energy and raw materials consumption. This move would be accompanied by a reduction in income tax and non-wage costs such as social security contributions. The market would thus be more efficient, energy—and material-intensive new production more expensive, labour-intensive repair work and reconditioning cheaper, and jobs would remain in the home country or region.

A number of more recent studies show clearly that an ecological tax reform would help to create jobs, and thereby could make a decisive contribution to reducing unemployment.

19

World Trade—The Next Challenge

On 15 December 1993 the world changed. My be not as dramatically as the moment when the Berlin Wall fell, but then unlike that very necessary demolition job, the success of the Uruguay Round was a work of construction. Like the destruction of the wall, though, its effects will be profound and lasting ones felt far beyond its immediate context. It will be seen as a defining moment in modern history.

The importance of the Round can be seen in terms of boost it gives to job creation; to development; to investment; to economic reform; to the rule of law and in many other ways besides. All of these benefits are real and important. But the true value of the whole is much, much more than the sum of these parts.

Put simply, governments came to the conclusion that the notion of a new world order was not merely attractive but absolutely vital; that the reality of the global market–whatever ambitions some of them may retain for regional integration–required a level of multilateral cooperation never before attempted.

No Losers in the Round

It has created a revolutionary framework for economic, legal and political cooperation. But now turn to the immediate results of the Round. Seeing them as a profit and loss account or a scorecard of winners and losers is to see them in static terms, as one-off conclusions with finite effects. This misses the point completely.

Every nation now needs an effective trading system, but especially so the small and poor. They have it. Everyone will also gain from the huge package of market access results even if they did not get every concession they were seeking from trading partners—it is the biggest market access deal ever negotiated.

However, the essence of the Uruguay Round's achievements is that they are dynamic. The new agreements, the new rules and structures it sets up—all mean a commitment to a continuing process of cooperation and reform of which the agreement in December was only the beginning.

Maintaining the liberalising momentum will call for continuing effort and vigilance by participating countries. But now their energy can be focused through the Round's greatest innovation; the new World Trade Organisation (WTO) in place of the improvised basis on which the GATT has operated for 45 years, trade will now have a permanent forum appropriate to its importance in the world economy.

Technically speaking, the WTO will oversee the implementation of the Round's results, administer all the agreements in goods, services and intellectual property, and manage the unified dispute settlement system. But beyond these administrative functions, it will raise the political profile of trade a profile which has already been lifted greatly by the Uruguay Round. The WTO will have regular instead of occasional—direct Ministerial involvement. It will have a clear mandate to act as a forum for further trade negotiations. Most of all it will complete the transition from a trading system which largely restricted itself to policies at the border to one which also covers most aspects of domestic policy-making affecting international competition in goods and services, as well as investment.

Through the WTO, the Round will change the way the world economy is shaped. But it is not the final victory over protectionism and unilateralism. Any premature rejoicing would have quickly been cut short by the evidence since 15 December that major economic powers are still ready to take the unilateral approach to trade problems. Arguments for protectionism based on the alleged threat of low-cost competition to production and jobs will not just fade away because the Round is a success. The seductive appeal of "beggar-thy-neighbour" policies is highlighted by the seemingly greater vigour of the lobbies for protectionism than the advocates of open markets.

These dangers—and the speed with which they have resurfaced—make the achievement of the Uruguay Round all the more important, and its successful implementation all the more urgent. Implementation requires more than mutual backslapping about what we have achieved. It requires now that the US, EU and Japan, in particular, rapidly obtain final authority to ratify and also take a lead in providing the WTO with the means to fulfil its mandate.

The success of the Round has come at a time when it is even more vitally needed than anyone could have guessed when it was launched in 1986. Old structures and alignments have been turned inside out in trade as in every other area of international relations. We face a world of change and challenge, in which the reinforced trading system will be a primary source of stability and security.

The developing countries including India have become enthusiastic supporters of the multilateral trading system and the Uruguay Round even if all their demands were not met by industrial countries. The reasons lie in the changing economic policies of many developing countries and the clearer appreciation of the value of the GATT system that has grown along with these changes.

The challenge of new issues in world trade will be a major one for the WTO. The new organisation has to consider issues such as the links between trade and the environment, international competition policy, trade and investment, and trade and labour standards. To say a few words about trade and the environment since it is one area in which GATT member countries have committed themselves already to a comprehensive new work programme. They decided on 15 December, in conjunction with the adoption of the results of the Uruguay Round negotiations, to draw up a work programme on trade and environment by the Ministerial meeting in Marrakesh. Environmental policy-making is one of the most rapidly evolving areas of national and international policy-making, and it is entirely appropriate that emphasis should be placed now in GATT/WTO on ensuring better policy coordination and multilateral cooperation over the linkages between trade and environment.

Permanent Negotiations

The Uruguay Round may well be the last of its kind, but this in no way means the end of multilateral trade negotiations. On the contrary, it means they become a permanent event. Ad hoc negotiating rounds were necessary mainly because the GATT lacked the mandate or the institutional basis to operate the multilateral system to the full on a continuous basis. Between rounds the GATT has tended to lose momentum, often at the very times when it was essential to make the most of the liberalising impulse. This has allowed protectionism and unilateralism to recover and regroup and meant that each round has to start by regaining lost ground.

The positive results of the Uruguay Round will redefine much more than assumptions about trade. If they are exploited with the same determination, courage and commitment that went into concluding the Round, they should mean nothing less than a new start for sustainable growth and a new system of collective economic security for the world.

But if the trading system is now up to the job of supporting multilateral cooperation on such a wide scale, do the other structures of economic cooperation still meet the bill? The establishment of the WTO will put trade and investment on a par—perhaps rather in advance—of cooperation in monetary and financial areas. The WTO will stand alongside its original Bretton Woods sisters, the IMF and the World Bank. The three institutions must learn to work together even more effectively and closely. For example, rather than each body conducting separate reviews of country policies, is there not a case to be made for a more integrated approach on country reviews? But that does not, on its own, add up to effective multilateral economic cooperation. The question really has to be asked seriously: are the G7, the OECD, the regional groupings adequate to provide that cooperation?

It is the next challenge of international economic leadership—the challenge of translating the common interest in global growth into a practical and effective mechanism for solving our common economic problems together. So, the Ministers meeting in Marrakesh is an historic event which will establish the World Trade Organisation and put in place the new multilateral trading system, they will be making not an end, but a beginning.

20

No Progress Without a Secular Society

Every day, women continue to be victims of rape, trafficking, acid-throwing, dowry deaths and other kinds of torture. At the opening of this new century, women are still not considered as equal human beings in many parts of the world, religion and patriarchy continue to have an all-encroaching hold on their lives, maintaining and justifying their age-old oppression. In some South Asian Societies, this hold is even increasing.

I do not believe that there can be real equality in a society dominated by religion. Western countries speak repeatedly about the necessity of economic development to alleviate poverty. But this is not enough. Some oil rich countries may be economically developed, but women are deprived of all rights. The supremacy of religion is incompatible with freedom of expression, women's rights and democracy. This is why I see religion as the main enemy of women's development.

We have to act on several fronts at once. First of all, improving access to education. In a society like Bangladesh, 80 per cent of women are illiterate. For centuries women have been taught they are the slaves of men. It is very hard to change their minds, to make them aware of their oppression, to give them a sense of their independence. This educational effort has to go hand in hand with a secular feminist movement in society. Such movements have to start within the country and they cannot take hold when people are uneducated and unaware of their oppression. I'm not sure you can accomplish much from the outside, except to expose in the media the atrocities women in all too many countries face in their day to day lives.

In some countries, this movement is emerging, but very timidly, and it has a slim margin of maneuver. It has the uphill task of fighting for the repeal of religious laws and the introduction of a uniform civil code. So far, it tends to be constituted by a few individual feminists who are forced to be diplomatic, to compromise with fundamentalists, be they men or women. But they are trying to change the system, step by step, and it will take a very long time. People are not yet ready to do away with religious laws that impact upon every aspect of society, from education and health to the workplace and the home.

For women's status to change, we also need enlightened leaders who believe in equality. In countries of South Asia women with a strong voice do not have the support of political leaders, whether they be men or women. Look at the countries in which women are in politics, or even heads of state. Does it follow that women in those countries are emancipated? Because of long-standing vested interests, such leaders continue to back measures that oppress women. They are not ideologically committed to changing these conditions. In South Asia, most of the women who become heads of state are religious, and like men, they adhere to the religious objectives of the establishment. Until a society is not based on religion and women and considered equal to men before the law, I do not think that politics will advance the cause of women.

Until a society is not based on religion and women are considered equal to men before the law, I do not think that politics will advance the cause of women. In Western countries, women are educated, they are treated equally, they have access to jobs. In these conditions, their participation in politics has a meaning.

Education, a secular feminist movement and leaders—both men and women—committed to equality and justice. This is what it will take to change the dire conditions which too many women still face today. It will take a very long time, but we are here to work towards that end.

21

Forests

The Earth's Lungs

The world's forest cover is shrinking. Over the past 50 years nearly half of the world's original forest cover has been lost—some 3 billion hectares. Each year another 16 million hectares of virgin forest are cut, bulldozed, or burned.

Between 1980 and 1995 the world lost some 180 million hectares of forest—an area the size of Indonesia. While developed countries had a net increase of 20 million hectares due to reforestation, this gain was more than offset by a net decrease of 200 million hectares in the developing world.

Forests have many functions of value both to humanity and to nature itself. Take away the trees, and the intricately linked ecosystem unravels. Forests absorb carbon dioxide and produce oxygen, anchor soils, regulate the water cycle, protect against erosion, and provide a habitat for millions of species.

Forest products are essential to the world economy, worth about US $ 400 billion annually in timber, pulp, paper, and fuel wood. Forest products other than wood, such as medicines, vegetables, and fruits, provide another US $ 20 billion and are growing in importance.

Healthy forests boost food production. Trees soak up and store water from season to season, slowly releasing moisture during dry periods. Without tree cover, water runs off faster during the tropical rainy season, carrying away valuable topsoil. A World Bank study found that the rate of soil loss was 10 times higher on forest lands where slash-and-burn shifting cultivation was practised than in undisturbed forests. One reason that agricultural yields have fallen in sub Sahran Africa is that vast amounts of forest cover have disappeared, hastening soil erosion and loss of soil nutrients.

Forest cover regulates climate, while destruction of forests contribute to global warming. Whereas living trees soak up and store carbon dioxide from the atmosphere trees that are cut down and burned release carbon into the atmosphere. In the last decade tropical deforestation has released large amounts of stored carbon—accounting for roughly one-quarter of the carbon dioxide emissions to the atmosphere due to human activity.

Pressures on Forests

Current demand for forests products may exceed the limits of sustainable consumption by 25 per cent. The developed world accounts for most of the demand for forest products. With just 16 per cent of the world's population, North America, Europe, and Japan consume two-thirds of the world's paper and paperboard and half its industrial wood. Demand for industrial wood products also has risen in developing countries, however, along with demand for fuel wood, the main energy source for many rural communities.

Throughout the 1990s many developing countries with rapid population growth had high rates of deforestation. Forest land was converted to agricultural use, and trees cut to provide housing and wood for fuel. Moreover developing countries stepped up exports of forests, products to meet the rising demand from developed countries.

The amount of forest area per capita fell by half between 1960 and 1995—reflecting both population growth and the disappearance of forests cover. In 1995 close to 1.7 billion people lived in countries with less than one-tenth of a hectare of forest cover per capita (83). By 2025, an estimated 4.6 billion people will live in such countries.

What Can Be Done?

As population grows and per capita consumption of forest products increases, countries must do more to manage forest resources on a sustainable basis. The following developments offer encouragement:

Technological Improvements: Technological improvements including use of recycled paper and paperboard, have substantially reduced the amount of pulp needed to produce paper. In 1970 paper and paperboard consisted of 80 per cent wood pulp. By 1997 more efficient production processes had reduced that figure to 56 per cent. As a direct result, the production of pulp for paper is expected to grow by just over 1 per cent a year over the next decade, about half the growth rate in the 1980s.

Forest Products Certification: Adopting a system that identifies forest products that come from sustainable managed forests could support efforts toward sustainability. As of 1998, about 10 million hectares of forest lands have been certified. Over 90 per cent of the certified area is in northern, temperature forests, mostly in Europe and North America. Close to 60 per cent of the entire certified area is in just two countries—Sweden and Poland—reflecting education and awareness campaigns in those countries. In tropical forests, where most of the destruction is taking place today, only tiny areas have been certified as providing sustainable yield.

Intergovernmental Responses: In 1995 the Intergovernmental Panel on Forests (IPF) was established in response to the 1992 Earth Summit. The IPF evolved into the inter governmental Forum on Forests in 1997, after the UN's five year review of the Earth Summit goals. The mission of the forum is to examine the underlying causes of deforestation and to help countries develop strategies that address them.

Efforts to advance an international legal convention on forests, which begin in 1990, have been shelved, however. Some observers believe that advancing such a convention would only codify the standards of a weak consensus and thus would be worse than no convention at all. Widespread opposition to a convention makes it unlikely that the issues will reach the negotiating table.

Instead, many organisations urge governments of countries with large forest resources to enforce existing legislation and to introduce more effective forest conservation initiatives close to 130 countries have developed or updated their National Forest programmes over the past decade.

While such initiatives are promising, they cannot be expected to half forest destruction completely. Millions of people rely on forest products for their livelihoods. Sustainable forest management will require not just enforcement of laws that project forests but also alternative sources of livelihood for many rural people.

22

Turning on the Heat

India's National Programme on Solar Cooking

Anyone who has ever watched a pot of water being boiled just by the sun is sure to have been impressed. High-quality solar cooker can reach temperatures over 200ºC. This temperature is more than sufficient to cook food, bake bread and heat up an iron for ironing clothes. As rural people in many parts of the world heavily depend on wood for preparing meals, solar cooking can also make an important contribution to saving our forests. But even after three decades of implementation, solar cookers have not evolved into commercially viable products that sell themselves. India is the country with the most experience in this field.

The principle behind solar cooking is as fascinating as it is simple: sun rays are converted to heat and conducted into the cooking pot. Solar cooking also has some practical advantages: solar power is inexhaustible, clean and free. By lessening their dependency on conventional fuels people can save money and non-renewable resources as well as the environment. The solar cookers often make use of a box or parabolic reflector to concentrate the sun's rays.

In India some 4,75,000 solar cookers were sold last year with the help of government grants and highly subsidised prices. That puts India way ahead of all other countries. In rural homes (70 per cent of the Indian population lives in rural areas) cooking accounts for a major share of total energy consumption. The available energy sources are firewood, crop residues and animal dung. In urban and semi-urban areas, gas, kerosene oil and coal are used for cooking purposes. The smoke emitted from these fuels pollutes the environment and the kitchen, affecting the health of the family members, especially the women. Fuel-wood is becoming scarce due to the depletion of forest.

Solar Energy is Abundant

Solar cooking has long been envisaged as a solution to mitigate these problems. After all, solar energy is abundantly available in most parts of the country. The daily average solar energy incidence ranges between five to seven kmwhr/m^2 and there are as many as 250 to 300 clear sunny days a year. On such days it is possible to cook both mid-day and evening meals in a solar cooker. It is, however, recognised that solar cooking cannot fully replace conventional fuels. The Government of India first initiated efforts in the early 1980s to popularise solar cooking devices all over the country in order to reduce dependency on conventional fuels.

National Programme Launched

A national programme on solar cooking was launched during 1981-82, which promoted above all the box-type cooker on account of its relative advantages. The concentrating types were not selected due to their high cost, the need for frequent tracking and the fast deterioration of reflecting surface etc. A subsidy of 33 per cent of the cost was granted by Central Government. In some states, an additional subsidy was also provided. To maintain the quality of the solar cookers being marketed, standard specifications were developed and given to all manufacturers and state agencies. Extensive efforts were also made to promote a wide network of manufacturers so that, over the years, around 55 manufacturers established units. The programme driven by the subsidy scheme was continued until 1994, when it was decided to adopt a market orientation and introduce new arrangements.

Studies to monitor practical benefits were conducted and revealed that while over 70 per cent of the owners were using their cookers, many did not use them frequently. The rest were not cooking with them at all due to climate problems, non-availability of open space, time constraints or cookers being out of order. Main requirements in the field of service were found to be the black-painting of tray and vessels, removal of moisture between glazings, replacement of broken glasses and prevention of hot air leakage. Shortcomings of the programme itself also became clear. As the manufacturers delivered the cookers to the state agencies who were selling them on, they were mainly interested in supplying cookers and gave insufficient attention to after-sale service for the product. They were not interested in developing their own sales and services network. This meant that customers could not get a model of their choice. All these factors finally led to the termination of the subsidy regime.

New Commercialisation Strategy

In order to give the programme a stronger market orientation, a new strategy was evolved in 1994 aimed at the commercialisation of solar cookers. Under this scheme, manufacturers were allowed to make modifications to the cooker design to make them more attractive and user-friendly. Sales were allowed both through state agencies and directly by manufacturers through their own network.

Certain negative trends have also emerged: Contrary to the original intention, it has become apparent that most solar cookers were being sold in cities and suburban areas. A price of 25 to 60 US dollars—depending on the model—is still too high for the rural population. Nevertheless, the programme focuses on commercial success in view of the excellent progress now being made. Th market-oriented programme is leading to the creation of independent distribution networks, better customer service and user-friendly models. However, commercialisation has, for the time being at least, brought higher prices and falling output. Low cost but durable models still need to be developed for wider dissemination of the technology in rural areas.

Sales Showrooms

A new initiative by the government is focusing on the establishment of showrooms for the sale and servicing of renewable energy products (including solar cookers) in major cities of the country. With financial help from the government they will offer over-the-counter sales of different renewable energy products, disseminate information and carry out repair and servicing of the equipment. These solar shops, which operate under the name of "Aditya" (meaning Sun in Sanskrit), allow manufacturers from all over the country to present their solar cookers and other products to the public. The average sale during the last five years have numbered 25,000.

To boost the sale of solar cookers and provide after sale services to users, a new scheme for self-employed workers (SEWs) has been introduced in 1999. Under this scheme, state agencies enlist a set of SEWs in their respective states who will receive training in the repair of solar cookers and in their proper use and preparation for various types of cooking. These SEWs will be recruited among unemployed youths with a technical qualification and experience in mechanical work. The scheme worker is to act as a link between the users and the manufacturers and banks. The SEW shall receive a nominal payment per cooker as a promotional incentive for selling more cookers in his area.

Never were these cookers more necessary than today. Wood burning still meets 15 to 18 per cent of primary energy consumption—more that nuclear and hydropower together. Greater demand for fuelwood is not only leading to desertification, it will also leave a growing number of people (the FAO puts the figure already at two billion) without enough energy to prepare themselves a regular hot meal.

❋❋❋

23

Between Wish and Reality

The Limited Potential of Solar Cookers

Efforts to promote the idea of using solar cookers have been made for decades, but despite great commitment they have failed. Nowhere has it come to self-sustaining commercial dissemination of these cookers. Above all, it has not been possible to reach; the main target group, the rural population. But that has not detracted from the fascination of using the sun to cook.

The Indian Experience

Most experience with solar cookers has been gathered in India. The National Physical Laboratory in New Delhi tested the efficiency of cooking boxes and concentrating cookers back in 1953. Large batches were produced at the beginning of the 1960s, but evidently without lasting success. That meant when in 1981 a national programme to disseminate cooking boxes was launched, it had to begin all over again. Over the course of time and with strong government promotion, 55 manufacturers began producing the units. Subsidies pushed the sales price down to half the production cost of US $ 60-70, and in low-income areas even down to US $ 15.

At the same time, the government ran a radio, television and newspaper advertising campaign to promote the cookers, and roped in prominent figures to endorse them. Other promotions featured cooking demonstrations in villages, and giving a solar cooker as a prize for couples that danced best at parties. About 1,20,000 cookers were sold in the way by 1990. But that was only a deceptive success. Random checks found that after a while most households used their solar cookers only occasionally. About 30 per cent no longer used them at all for various reasons.

The results were especially poor in the villages. A survey of rural energy consumption in six Indian federal states in 1996 found that of 51,000 households only 70 possessed a solar cooker. At the same time, the survey also refuted the oft-repeated prejudice that the people opposed innovations and rejected them even when they were useful. After all, 6,200 of the households surveyed had bought a pressure cooker because they cooked faster and used less fuel.

India is now making a fresh attempt to propagate solar cookers. According to the Ministry of Non-conventional Energy Sources, almost 500,000 highly subsidised cookers were sold in 1998. It is not clear how better results are to be achieved this time. The programme director is surprised that most of the cookers are sold in towns rather than in rural areas, although based on earlier experience nothing else was to be expected.

Socio-Cultural Factors

The causes of the only modest success of solar cooking equipment lie less in the technical sector than in the socio-cultural, socio-economic and psycho-social area. This profound-sounding formulation identifies what is basically a simple fact. Solar cookers function, but they cannot replace the customary cooker. Even in arid zones the sun does not always shine, and in the mornings and evenings cooking must anyway be done by customary methods. That means solar cookers are a supplementary way of cooking that saves fuel.

Experience has shown, however, that it saves at most one-third of usual fuel consumption. That is not fundamental progress for a household, only a degree of improvement. It is quite different from the situation in, for example, the photovoltaic (PV) sector, which enables completely new things such as electric light and radio reception. So it is not surprising that small, portable PV systems are very much in demand even among Tibetan nomads.

By contrast, a solar cooker is rated by purely economic criteria. Savings of time or money are balanced against the cost of the unit and its limits. Not all meals can be cooked on a solar cooker, preparation takes longer, and the cooking process can no longer be controlled as one like because it is determined by the amount of energy the sun offers. These disadvantages are not due to any particular shortcomings of the solar cooker as such which could be remedied by further development, but to the vagaries of the sun itself as a source of energy.

Tibet as a Special Case

The only region in the world where solar cookers are firmly established is Tibet. A total of 70,000 to 1,00,000 units are estimated to be in use among a population of two million. But Tibet is a special case in which several favourable conditions for hours of sunshine per year, or an average of eight hours per day, and the intensity of its solar radiation is so high that with only a few exceptions solar cooking is possible throughout the whole year. Since sunshine in Tibet means almost always direct radiation, concentrators with parabolic reflectors are used.

On the other hand, Tibet has an extreme shortage of other fuels. Firewood in simple not available. There are hardly any trees in the mountains. Other traditional sources of fuel such as shrub, yak dung or turf are also extremely scarce and hardly available for the inhabitants of the three cities of Lhasa, Shigatse and Gyantse. They are dependent on cylinder gas or kerosene that must be brought in over thousands of kilometers from China and is correspondingly expensive.

Local eating habits also favour the use of solar cookers. For the yak butter tea Tibetans drink incessantly throughout the day a household needs a continual supply of hot water. The concentrator cookers, which can boil five litres of water in 15-20 minutes, are highly suitable for that. They are also used to cook rice, but very little for other meals. The structure of Tibetan housing areas is another factor favouring solar cookers, their enclosed courtyards and flat roofs providing, plenty of space for setting them up. All that has resulted in almost every urban household possessing a solar cooker. But use of the cookers in rural areas is much less widespread because the people have less money and transporting the heavy units to villages is difficult and expensive.

Regional Contribution

Favourable conditions like those in Tibet are seldom to be found anywhere else. Viewed realistically, solar cookers are not the global solution to the firewood crisis. At best, they make a regional contribution. Portraying the dissemination of solar cookers as a benedictory concept also does not help it further. Most of the solar cooker enthusiasts are still far from this insight. The World Solar Cooking and Food Processing Conference, held in Varese, Italy, last October and attended by 300 experts from 64 countries, once again provided abundant material in support of solar cookers. The conference's final statement said: "Solar cooking has the potential to be one of the most significant contributions to solving the firewood problem."

24

Unemployment in the Poor and Rich Worlds

Different Causes, But Converging Policies?

In view of the magnitude of global unemployment, all the customary formulas offered by economists against mass unemployment—the basic socio-economic problem of modern times—appear to be quackery. Neither quantitative, nor any kin of 'qualitative', growth will be able to eliminate the disastrous worldwide lack of jobs. For ecological reasons it is impossible to include 800 million or more unemployed in the production process through corresponding growth. The resulting increase in global Gross Domestic Product would require consumption of natural resources, energy and the environment which, given even the greatest possible productivity in those sectors, could not even be sustained for two or three decades.

In addition, aiming to achieve full employment through growth will be ever more difficult even in the rich economies. For it is most likely that work productivity will continue to rise worldwide. Countries such as China, which are in the initial phase of modernisation, are still producing at a relatively still low productivity rate. But that is precisely why they can achieve notable increases in productivity in a short time by importing technology from highly-developed countries. The advantage of rapid 'catch-up rationalisation', however, is being bought at the cost of rising unemployment and progressive impoverishment.

Employment Through Redistribution of Work

The notion that jobs can at some time be created for 800-900 million unemployed who will work 35 or even 40 hours a week at the productivity level of the highly-developed countries of four or five decades ago is absurd. The only realistic possibility of eliminating the world's unemployment problem is by far-reaching redistribution of work and income. The change needed for that demands fundamentally new concepts of prosperity: a reflection on the philosophy of the 'life of happiness'. 'New concepts of prosperity' means that technological progress would no longer be used mainly to deliver rising per capita incomes and excessive consumption. Instead, given a sufficient material standard of living, the quality of life would be improved primarily by shortening working hours. It is about, so to speak, assigning instrumental good sense new goals. Plus reshaping socio-economic conditions in such a way that the politicians will again be compelled to orient themselves on the good of the community and humanistic values instead of filling the pockets of the wealthy. It is sheer ideology, although very persuasive, to cite 'globalisation' and its alleged 'iron laws' in defaming the welfare state, full employment and social justice as out-of-date wishful thinking. A return to the state-guided social competitive system as practised during the first decades after the Second World War is possible just as it was politically feasible to make the transition from the old order of unfettered, ruthless capitalism to the mixed economies of the social market economy types. So it is a matter of restoring the proven structures of a mixed economic system.

However, in contrast to the first postwar decades it is now not sufficient to regenerate nation-sate interventionism. Appropriate international regualtions are required. Above all, it will depend upon reversing the new laissez-faire developments in international economic relationships which today are subsumed under the buzzword 'globalisation'. That is, to oppose over-liberalisation and its disastrous social and inhuman impacts. It will depend on the broad mobilisation of the losers in the process of globalisation whether the necessary fundamental change of course can still be made in time before a catastrophe. In particular, the new myth must be opposed that declares globalisation as a kind of law of nature and thus suggests resignation and adaptation to an allegedly unavoidable process of destruction of social and human achievements.

Mass Unemployment in the Poor Economies

The employment problems in the rich and the poor hemispheres differ not only in their magnitude, but also in their causes. The wretched condition of the poor economies is due above all to historical reasons: colonialism and, in the post-colonial era, the constraints to independent development imposed by the hegemonic influence of the rich industrial states. The waste of scarce resources by international and civil wars, and the dictatorships with their upperclass luxury consumption and inefficient, thus development—obstructing exploitation structures—often supported by the industrialised nations, have for a long time repressed and in many cases destroyed autonomous development potential. The colonial and post-colonial distortion also contributed at least indirectly to the current population problems of the poor countries. The politically inflicted mass poverty and under-development stabilised or in fact brought about economic, socio-psychological and ideological mechanisms which oppose an effective population policy. As we know, the average educational level in many developing countries, especially among women, is too low to give a modern population policy a chance of success. Mass unemployment in the poor countries is the result of poverty. In this respect, it is about a production-side problem: too few resources, to little real and human capital, and the inefficient, unproductive use of much of the anyway limited added value of society. The picture is totally different in the rich countries—the over-production economies.

Unemployment in Over-Production Systems

The main cause of mass unemployment in the industrialised nations has nothing to do with shortages. It is a phenomenon of surplus. Greater possibilities of production can no longer be used 'sufficiently profitably because the required demand is lacking. Production is done for profit. The necessary collateral condition is the satisfying of consumer needs. Employment is not even such a condition, but only a side effect which lapses immediately when labour-free production is technically possible. Thus, national income must be shared among wages and profits (or income from property). Profit is the difference between earnings and costs. Earnings depend upon demand. Macro-economic costs consist mainly of wages and salaries (including social security contributions). These definitive connections mean that profit can be made only if overall demand is greater than the total cost of labour. But in the final analysis this demand can only come from the profit-earners themselves. In his book, a Treatise on Money, Keynes described this nexus as the theory of the Widow's cruse. Under capitalistic conditions, labour is only sought or hired if profit can be earned with it. But as making a profit depends upon the demand for consumption and investment by the shareholders, it can be seen that the degree of employment is determined by the demand behaviour of the class that receives income from property. In this respect, the widespread belief that greater investment also leads to more employment, namely via the effect of investment in demand, is right.

Lower Wages Mean Lower Demand

The lower the level of wages, and given an unchanged total demand, the greater are the profits that can be made. But it is more likely that in the case of falling wages the overall demand will also drop. For stabilising total demand would require the recipients of income from property to increase their spending on consumption and/or investment to the degree to which wages and the consumption based on them fell.

During the last 10 to 15 years the development of profits in most industrialised nations has been very favourable. But profits would have grown more strongly if the demand of the shareholder had been much greater. This would have created more employment at the same time. Thus, it can be assumed that the profits are simply too high for the shareholders to be able to go in for meaningful consumption or make profitable investments. That is the reason for the extreme redirection of capital from fixed assets to portfolio investment. The growth of speculative (unproductive) financial transactions during the 1980s and 1990s (buzzword: casino capitalism), corresponded with a relatively weak formations of real capital.

Wage rises, of course, narrows the scope for profit. But precisely this effect stimulated efforts to improve the profit situation not only by investment in rationalisation, but also by investment in expansion aimed at the growing mass purchasing power. Since more is being invested, the profit mass also is growing according to the principle of the Widow's cruse. Too low wages, as it were, relieve the shareholders of the pressure to innovate and invest and allow them to earn their profits too easily. That is the real message of the 'purchasing power theory' of wages.

Over-accumulation and Under-consumption

Over-production has two different causes which, however, mostly occur in tandem. They are over-investment, or creation of over-capacities, on the one hand, and lack of demand due to relative saturation and an absence of mass purchasing power on the other. But the main reason for mass unemployment in the rich hemisphere currently lies on the demand side. During the first three decades after the Second World War supply and demand rose in relative balance. Economic fluctuations showed up as temporary declines in generally positive GDP growth rates. These decades of (dynamic) balance of growth are often described today as the era of 'Fordism'. Its essential feature is that rising wages ensure continuing growth of consumption, so that equally growing profits also flow relatively continuously into investments to expand capacity and create jobs. The label 'Fordism' expresses the 'simple' view of the theory for the buying power of wages which is said to have been propagated by Henry Ford I. This was that his workers should earn enough to be able to buy the cars they made.

The astonishingly balanced development of supply and demand from 1950 to the mid-1970s was due above all to postwar reconstruction and the pent-up demand of consumers who were starved by wartime economy shortages. This stimulated positive investment sentiment, and high investments brought at the same time high profits. The postwar growth that led within a short time to full employment was also linked with growth in productivity, which on multi-year average was more than twice that of the crisis period of the last 25 years. Thus, the so-called employment threshold (the GDP growth rate point at which employment growth begins) was much higher in those days than it is now, although there was full employment over a longer period. This simple fact opposes the thesis often propounded today that mass unemployment is above all related to rationalisation. It is not rationalisation per se, that is, progress that boosts productivity, which is the evil. The problem is that the mistakes in distribution policy which are rooted in capitalistic structures result in increases in supply encountering insufficient demand for goods, whereby the demand for labour drops. However, the fact that demand policy contradicts the requirements of a social ethic that is ecologically responsible and right for the interests of the poor countries was already spelled out. So if a demand-oriented growth policy is practised at all, it should be designed to be as environmentally compatible as possible. After all, there are possibilities for that, such as by expanding the production of services that spare resources. A one-hour driving lesson costs more energy than one hour of ballet instruction.

The politically initiated and implemented over-liberalisation and surrender of social prosperity to global competition since the 1970s, which reproduces the old self-destructive mechanism of laissez faire, have during the last two decades markedly accelerated the crisis development inherent in the system.

Summing Up, It is Noted that

- Full employment in the rich economies would certainly be possible by means of demand policy, but only at a high cost to the environment that is concomitant with high growth rates;
- The growth policy of the rich countries impairs the poor economies' possibilities of medium to long-term growth, since these are falling back ever further in the competition for ever scarcer and thus ever more expensive resources;
- The environmental collapse currently expected for the third or fourth generation after us, which obviously also will trigger a collapse of the world economy and—probably ahead of that—armed conflicts which today are hardly imaginable, would happen very much sooner if economic growth were to be increased to such a degree that it would bring full employment worldwide;
- In the long term, the problem of global unemployment and global poverty can only be solved by a policy of massive redistribution, and in fact a redistribution of work and income, whereby increases in productivity must be used mainly or only for shortening working hours. That is a demand, which appears to be utopian. But utopias of today often have the quality of scripting the reality of tomorrow.

❄ ❄ ❄

25

Tapping the Market
Can Private Enterprise Supply Water to the Poor?

Over 170 million people have no access to clean water in urban areas throughout the world. Inefficient operation of state owned water companies is at the root of this injustice: gross over-staffing and political interference in tariff-setting have starved utilities of the resources needed to expand piped networks to impoverished areas.

The failure of the supply-driven approach has led to public private partnership (PPPs) designed to shift water utilities towards a demand-driven approach. Have these changes been accompanied by improved access to clean, affordable water for the urban poor? Has PPP improved equity in urban water supply? Are the new private sector operators addressing the needs of the urban poor in practice? This article examines the extent to which the urban poor have benefited or not from this newly emerging institutional arrangement.

The 'public' approach typically provides unclean water sporadically. It requires expensive, highly educated professionals, significant subsidies and tends to service clients on high and middle incomes whilst changing low tariffs. International financial institutions have failed to enable the public water suppliers to improve performance, either through massive investment in engineering, or through capacity building and institutional development.

At the other extreme is an efficient, demand driven, customer-oriented approach, the 'small scale independent providers', delivering water to cities' inhabitants, with near 100 per cent bill collection efficiency. Promoting local employment and servicing the poor, this approach has, until recently, been ignored by water sector professionals. Lacking regulatory oversight, however, their prices are typically 10 to 20 times higher than those paid by high-income consumers connected to the network. Which of these providers are most effective at serving the poor? The starting point is to recognise the evidence suggesting that the urban poor are prepared to pay to meet their survival and convenience needs for water.

Notwithstanding the rhetoric to the contrary by some trade unions and NGOs, initial results from larger cities indicate that the efficiency of 'privatised' water utilities has improved markedly: leakages are down and net revenue is up through improved billing and collection and reduction in personnel. Whether this is due to the alleged benefits of private sector investment or the freedom of foreign operators to manage without being beholden to employee and entrenched political interests is not yet clear.

Has the Extension of the Network to Poor Communities Been Speeded Up?

Concession contracts require private operators to meet coverage targets. But the decisions on the direction of network expansion to meet targets are usually left to the operators as regulatory bodies are usually formed after contract signing. So are poor communities given priority? Technical criteria based on cost-effectiveness in the construction of main pipes, commercial criteria based on pressure from property developers, and political criteria based on vote-winning tactics may all conflict with social criteria based on the pressing needs of poor communities.

Is the Cost of Household Connection Affordable by the Poor?

Even where operators do give priority to extending the piped network into poor communities, difficult issues arise over the financing of secondary pipelines, household connections and meter installation. Techniques are evolving to reduce the cost of connection so as to ensure affordability for all. These may take the form of tripartite arrangements whereby the public sector provides grants for the purchase of materials, community groups provide voluntary labour, and the private operator provides technical assistance. NGOs may contribute by providing crucial skills in team management and local understanding not usually found in the bureaucratic culture of public sector institutions or the techno-professional culture of private water companies.

Is the Water Tariff Affordable by the Poor?

Even where poor communities have been connected, there is no assurance that householders can afford the water charges. Many have no job security or regular income. Billing arrangements need to be shortened from the monthly norm to fit the short-term financial horizon imposed by household poverty.

Property-based tariff structures still discriminate against the poor by providing far cheaper water per litre for high-income households consuming large volumes for swimming pools and sprinkler systems. Reforms should positively discriminate in favour of the poor, with some cross-subsidisation from richer to poorer households. However, where the initial life-line block is greater than average monthly domestic water use by the poor (perhaps over 6m^3 per household a month), middle income groups benefits the most. A single volumetric tariff for domestic consumers with subsidies aimed at facilitating water connections rather than consumption is now being recommended.

This article focuses on the three major challenges for the sector in the new millennium:

- First it is crucial to develop regulatory skills to oversee this affordable expansion. The key capacity constraints facing municipalities—usually the public sector partners in PPPs;
- Second is the need to incorporate the skills of small-scale independent providers;
- Thirdly it is important to move beyond the metropolitan capitals, to where cross-subsidies are more achievable, and address the water needs of the urban poor in the myriad of secondary towns in the south.

26

The World Bank Needs Innovative Theory

The World Bank's macro-economic assumptions disregard many issues relevant to development. These include, for instance, population growth and income distribution. Endogenous growth models are better suited to analyse complex interactions than the conventional tools of neoclassic and post-Keynesian economics.

The World Bank is officially committed to sustainable development. Yet its own policy does not adhere to this principle. Structural adjustment programmes and poverty reduction strategies still conflict with social and ecological goals. One reason for the poor sustainability record is the World Bank's outdated theoretical approach based on neoclassic and post-Keynesian ideas.

Both are incompatible with sustainability. Neoclassic understanding of sustainability rests on the belief that technological progress automatically leads to a more efficient use of resources and, accordingly, to less ecological degradation.

For several reasons, post-Keynesian models are similarly incompatible with the principle of sustainability. First of all, they produce analyses for the short term. Typically, merely two periods are considered, which is inadequate for designing a growth process in general and even more so for a sustainable path to development. Moreover, these models also disregard distribution because they only take aggregated quantities into account.

World Bank economists, however, still work with country-specific variants of the post-Keynesian Revised Minimum Standard Model, although it is academically outdated and cannot deal with the complexity of development processes. The model's merits are that it is easy to understand and apply. In addition, little information on the behaviour of the economic actors is required. The World Bank determines the volume of its loans on the basis of such calculations. In addition to the transfer of these sums, the bank believes that measures to promote growth are necessary. These are expected to be in line with the Washington Consensus approach of privatisation, deregulation and liberalisation.

The structural and stabilisation measures that the World Bank economists implement are thus based on theoretical models which are incompatible with the principle of sustainability and which they, at most, supplement with cushioning elements. The obvious alternative would be to apply more recent approaches of endogenous growth theory. After all, economic growth is a precondition for sustainable development. Endogenous growth models are very diverse, so one cannot speak of an integrated and comprehensive theory. However, all endogenous models share the attempt to explain growth without recourse to exogenous factors. While the basic model of endogenous growth theory was developed for industrialised nations, it can be adapted to situations typical of developing countries. This gives an idea of the complex interrelatedness of economic phenomena.

Complex Interactions

These manifold links clearly serve to illustrate the shortcomings of the World Bank. For example, the IMF and the World Bank call for the immediate opening of national economies to world trade. By contrast, endogenous growth models suggest assessing free trade's benefits for developing countries more diligently. Trade liberalisation only presents an opportunity to increase long-term growth rates in developing countries when pursued in a differentiated way respecting specific needs of countries and sectors. Otherwise, there is a risk of economies specializing solely on low-technology goods, which, in turn, means forsaking long-term innovation.

Complementary measures are necessary if developing countries are to take advantage of liberalisation. Education, enhancement of communications and transport infrastructure and special mechanisms for the transfer of knowledge from advanced to developing countries (such as on-the-job-training, imitation of existing technologies and foreign direct investment) are important determinants for economic development. The level of education in a developing country is particularly significant. If a national economy has too little human capital, opening the markets mostly results in minor or even negative growth effects. Empirical studies support these statements.

Population growth is a serious obstacle to development. In many poor regions, it puts the already overburdened education and health systems under additional stress. Traditional economics theory, however, ignores the significance of fertility. Endogenous growth models can take family planning into account and link birth rates to social security systems as well as to environmental aspects. Doing so leads to developmental insights. For instance, short-term social cushioning measures, such as those implemented frequently by the World Bank and its partners to reduce the negative impacts of programme-tied loans, do not suffice for a positive development process. By contrast, long-term social security measures (such as introducing a pension scheme) contribute to reducing fertility.

Poverty Stalls Growth

Incomes in developing countries are mostly distributed

very unevenly. The World Bank, so far, does not view this as an important obstacle to development. At any rate, the widespread thesis that, in the wake of economic development, inequality first increases and then decreases by itself has empirically been shown to be wrong. Endogenous growth models under pin this finding in theoretical terms. Unequal income distribution results in too little investment in training, the consequences of which impede growth.

Endogenous models are also useful from an ecological viewpoint. According to neoclassic environmental and resources theory, external effects of noxious emissions and over-exploitation of resources must be internalised in order to ensure long-term economic growth. Instruments in tune with the market, such as taxes or certificates, are better suited to do so than strict governmental regulation. Even these findings are not yet paid enough attention in the Country Assistance Strategies in which the World Bank lays down short-to medium-term development strategies.

Endogenous growth theory contributes to analyzing the complex interactions of sustainable development. Even if most of the recommendations are well established in the critique of developmental practice, formal theoretical analyses help to avoid the arbitrariness of policy statements. Future research must show how to develop a user-friendly, comprehensive. Building on a profound analysis of development determinants, it will be possible to draft country specific development strategies in line with sustainability principles. These should be reflected in the conditionalities of programme-tied loans. To ensure consistent implementation of sustainable development policy, the World Bank must update its theoretical models. Endogenous growth theory provides a starting point.

27

Making the Multilateral System Work

International institutions are, as yet, too weak to ensure the provision of global public goods. It is not enough to merely defend the multilateral system against attacks. Its shortcomings must be acknowledged in order to find ways to a better future.

Nation states cannot establish security, prosperity and freedom on their own. In a globally networked world, constant policy failure looms unless there is cross-border cooperation. Yet instead of a multilateral drive to shape globalisation, we are witnessing a manifest crisis of multilateralism. This is not only a question of the Iraq war or of stagnation in the cases of the World Trade Organisation and the Kyoto Protocol. With good reason, critics of multilateralism point to the international system's bureaucratic Molochs, the rapid spread of institutions and the (frequently ineffective) proliferation of international conferences, decision and agendas. Moreover, elected politicians fear that the trend towards making decisions in systems of international negotiation will rob parliaments of their legitimate political power.

Talk of mulitlateralism's failure, however, might yet prove premature. The US government is now learning that, while it can win wars single-handedly, it, nevertheless, depends on alliances and the legitimatising authority of UN in order to establish peace, security and democracy. Perhaps, the shock of Cancun will soon lead to a willingness of the industrialised nations to compromise in the agricultural sector. A collapse of the world trade system would definitely not suit them.

Yet even if the pressure of global problems were to turn into a motor for multilateralism, that in itself would not iron out the weaknesses of the existing multilateral system. Shortcomings are becoming ever more apparent as the relevance of international coordination for national societies increases. Whoever believes that multilateralism is necessary must name its problems. As in the European Union, a lack of institutional reform is threatening to result in an incapacity to act.

It is not enough merely to defend the present institutions against the attacks of unilateralism. The prerequisites of a more effective multilateralism must yet be fulfilled. International coordination means designing policy in complex negotiating systems without the institutionally embedded hierarchies known in national government systems. This implies a host of problems—such as the great number of participants, decisions based on the lowest common denominator, the length of the negotiating processes and, not least, the manifold opportunities powerful actors have to evade international rules.

For international development cooperation, the efforts and debates concerning budget financing, programme assistance and coordinated sectoral projects by the donor community are similar relevance. The great crises of human kind cannot he mastered by single projects that are both costly and small-scale.

An agenda to strengthen multilateralism in development cooperation must go beyond these piecemeal approaches. Global policy needs a coherent structure of global governance.

Therefore the agenda should include the following, certainly conflict-prone, questions:

- How can the effectiveness and efficiency of multilateral development organisations be strengthened'? Which organisations have operational capacities? Which organisations should focus on coordinating, moderating or initiating programmes and agenda-setting'?
- How can sector-oriented multilateral organisations (such as the WTO, the World Health Organisation and the United Nations Environment Programme) contribute to getting a grip on trans-sector problems (such as climate change, disintegrating societies and population growth)? How can contradictions within the multilateral system's fragmented rules be overcome?
- How is overlap-stemming from multiple jurisdictions and parallel agendas within the multilateral system—be avoided? How can the cooperation of organisations be improved on the basis of their respective specialisation advantages? Which organisations or special programmes have become redundant and should be discontinued?
- How can actors (not only governments) from developing countries become responsible and appropriately represented players in the international system—especially in the World Bank and the International Monetary Fund? The buzzwords of experts are voice, capacity-building and power-sharing. Reforms are necessary to increase the effectiveness and legitimation of the institutions. On the other hand, The actors in the industrialised nations must not withdraw from these institutions as that would degrade them to scarcely effective discussion forums as has happened, for instance, to the UN Conference on Trade and Development (UNCTAD).
- How can internationally agreed standards (such as, for instance, the central norms of the International Labour Organisation) actually be enforced? Otherwise

multilateral institutions will remain toothless. What options are there for imposing sanctions? So far, due to the modus operandi of international law, powerful countries that flout international rules have been less hampered in their actions than actors who violate rules in the context of constitutionally regulated states. International agreements often lack mechanisms to punish rule infringements.

- What minimum standards should apply in future with respect to accountability, transparency and participation by societal actors? Anti-globalisation movements, civil societies accustomed to democracy, and parliaments claim the right to participate and cannot be simply disregarded.

The list of the challenges could easily go on. We are, indeed, dealing with Herculean tasks. For day-to-day politics, this is not a field that promises the quick score of "merit points", But whoever is concerned with the future of global society will have to come to grips with the difficult fundamentals and preconditions of a more effective multilateralism. Europe's national governments and the European Commission must ask themselves whether they have appropriate strategies for the future of multilateral organisations and whether they provide them with adequate resources.

Most likely, pioneer groups and progressive "coalitions of the willing" (frequently also called "Iikeminded states") will more and more often lead the way by seeking solutions to world problems even if other countries do not follow suit. It is about linking governments with other actors that want to forge ahead quickly in this field.

28

Climate Politics After Kyoto

Solidarity Understood Correctly

The Kyoto Protocol does not do enough to protect humankind from climate change. Additional binding reduction targets for greenhouse gases are necessary and they must also apply to important developing and transition countries. So far, these countries have been treated as a uniform group. In future, different rules will have to be used according to varying capabilities and different exposures to risk.

The Kyoto Protocol climate protection came into force internationally in February. At its core are binding commitments for industrialised countries to restrict their greenhouse gas emissions. This is an important step—however, it is only the first one in coming to terms with the challenge of the century: climate protection. The reduction targets of five per cent on average for advanced nations established so far are insufficient. Moreover, there are no obligations yet for developing and transition countries, which emit almost half of the greenhouse gases worldwide.

At the climate summit in Buenos Aires the European Union tried to kick-start negotiations on the further development of the Kyoto Protocol with moderate success. While the negotiations in the run-up to Kyoto were already quite difficult, the new phase of international climate politics that is just beginning presents even greater obstacles. Apart from reintegrating the climate—desperado USA into the international process, future negotiations will have to involve several transition and developing countries.

However, these countries point to the rich nations' historic responsibility for ongoing climate change. They are afraid their economic development might be slowed down. Meanwhile, many of the poorer developing countries are particularly vulnerable. Due to their geographical location, economic structure and weak financial and technical capacities, they are virtually, helplessly exposed to the consequences of the greenhouse effect. Therefore, future negotiations must break the "North-South" grid as well as find an adequate differentiation for the very heterogeneous countries of the "South".

The central theme of our work was the principle of solidaity. This implies that weak countries should be supported when tackling the effects of climate change. As started in Article 2 of the Framework convention of Climate Change, humankind's "dangerous" interference with the climate must be stopped. This means that global warming must be restricted to, at most, two centigrades above pre-industrial temperatures. Any warming above this level would threaten human existence in many regions. The cultural survival of local communities and the physical integrity of the weak and powerless would be acutely endangered.

Mitigation Becomes a Negotiation Topic

Even in keeping to this two degree mark, which the European union has adopted, impact of climate change, which is already noticeable now, would be aggravated further. The first conclusion of our team therefore is that future negotiations can no longer deal merely with combating the causes of the problem by redusing emissions. Talks have to go further and contribute to limiting damage. Measures to adapt to climate change, particularly in the case of very vulnerable countries, must play a central role.

In terms of finance, technology and personnel, many developing countries are in no position to adequately handle the negative consequences of climate change. They need transfer payments. Financing mechanisms that correspond to the "polluter pays" principle are inevitable—and introducing them is a precondition to move ahead with preventive measures. Developing countries will only be prepared to accept reduction targets for emissions if the industrialised countries contribute (financially) to adapting to climate change. All summed up, however, reduction and prevention of greenhouse gases also serve adaptation programmes. The more effectively climate protection is implemented, after all, the lower the costs for adapting to the climate change will be—not to mention irreversible effects of climate change, such as the extinction of animal and plant species and the melting of glaciers.

If climate change is to be limited to two degrees celsius on average globally humankind's emissions must peak by 2020, drop to half level reached in the 1990s by the middle of this century and then continue to decrease. There is widespread agreement among politicians, scientists civil society actors on the necessity of emission reductions the difficulties begin with question of which countries are to contribute. When does their obligation begin and what extent does it have?

The Kyoto Protocol retains the categories outlined in the Framework Convention on Climate Change. Accordingly, the advanced Western nations and the former Soviet block form one group(Annex countries) and the rest of the World the second group (Non-Annex I countries). This is not practical in the long term.

The Kyoto Protocol defines negotiated reduction obligations among the parties of the first group. Given the increasing contribution of the "rest of the world" to global emission levels, future regulations must also engage several transition and developing countries. To do so, it is necessary to differentiate more strongly between these countries—according to their capabilities and circumstances.

Criteria for Differential Treatment

In order to reflect the country—specific conditions in a fair manner, our proposal consider three criteria:

- the potential to reduce greenhouse gases;
- the capacity to finance reduction measures; and
- the responsibility for climate change.

In view of these criteria, the Non-Annex I countries obviously differ greatly. As a matter of course, all countries with the lowest emissions per capita are included. However, so are several countries with the highest emissions per capita world wide—Qatar, for example. All least developed countries (LDC) fall into the category, but so do countries such as Singapore, with a per capita income well above the average of the industrialised countries. Obviously, it does not make sense to treat these countries as equals in climate talks.

If the "Non-Annex countries" are differentiated according to the three criteria mentioned above, four groups can be identified:

- "Newly industrialising countries" (NIC);
- Rapidly industrializing developing countries" (RIDC);
- Other developing countries" (ODC);
- "Least developed countries"(LDC).

COUNTRY GROUPS

Newly Industrialised Countries"—NICs

Bahrain, Brunei, Cuba, Kazakhastan, South Korea, Kuwait, Qatar, Saudi Arabia, Singapore, Suriname, Trinidad and Tobago, Turkmenistan, United Arab Emirates, Uzbekistan.

"Rapidly Industrialising Developing Countries"—RIDs

Algeria, Antigua and Barbuda, Argentina, Bahamas, Barbodos, Belize, Bosnia and Herzegovina, Botswana, Brazil,

Chile, China, Colombia, Costa Rica, Cyprus, Dominican Republic, El Salvador, Fiji, Grenada, Guyana, Iran, Jordan, Malaysia, Malta, Mauritius, Mexico, Oman, Panama, Peru, Philippines, Saint Kitts and Nevis, Saint Lucia, Saint Vincent and Grenadines, South Africa, Thailand, Tunisia, Uruguay.

Other Developing Countries—ODCs

Armenia, Azerbaijan, Bolivia, Cameroon, Congo, Cook Islands, Cote d'lovire, Dominica, Ecuador, Egypt, Gabon, Georgia, Ghana, Honduras, India, Indonesia, Jamaica, Kenya, Kyrgyzstan, Libya, Macedonia, FYR, Moldova, Mongolia, Morocco, Namibia, Nicaragua, Nigeria, Pakistan, Papua New Guinea, Paraguay, Seychelles, Sri Lanka, Swaziland, Syria, Tajikistan, Venezuela, Vietnam, Zimbabwe.

Least Developed Countries—LDCs

Afghanistan, Angola, Bangladesh, Benin, Bhutan, Burkina Faso, Burundi, Cambodia, Cape Verde, Central African Republic, Chad, Comoros, Democratic Republic of Congo, Djibouti, Equatorial Guinea, Eritrea, Ethiopia, Gambia, Guinea, Guinea-Bissau, Haiti, Kiribati, Laos, Lesotho, Liberia, Madagascar, Malawi, Maldives, Mali, Mauritania, Mozambique, Myanmar, Nepal, Niger, Rwanda, Samoa, Sao Tome and Principe, Senegal, Sierra Leone, Solomon Islands, Somalia, Sudan Tanzania, Togo, Tuvalu, Uganda, Vanuatu, Yemen, Zambia.

We are not interested in splitting the negotiating group of the "G 77 and China" politically. But solidarity among these countries requires that those which are better off make a contribution to global climate protection on a different scale than, for example, the LDCs. Only in this way can the group retain its important unity in negotiations with the advanced countries and, at the same time, tackle the climate problem.

What would the climate protection obligations of the different country groups look like in concrete terms? We propose the following rules:

- The potential to reduce emissions should determine binding reduction targets. This potential arises from the emission intensity of a country (CO_2 emitted per unit of the gross domestic product) and from the emissions per capita. This line of action would guarantee a cost efficient climate regime, since emissions would be reduced wherever the potential for doing so was highest. This does not necessarily mean, however, that the countries, concerned would be liable to fund all necessary measures. Certainly the industrial countries would have to contribute too;
- Obligations to finance climate protection would have to derive from the respective capacity of a country. This capacity could be measured against the average income and the Human Development Index. Countries with a higher capacity—mainly industrialised countries—would have to support those with lower capacity;
- To what extent obligations become binding should ultimately depend on a country's contribution to climate change. The accumulated emissions since 1990 could serve as a suitable indicator. At that time, the United Nations had already identified the greenhouse effect as a human-made problem.

These rules would mean that the advanced industrialised countries, and to a somewhat lesser degree also the former planned economies, would have to take on absolute, binding reduction targets going far beyond Kyoto.

Moreover, these Annex-I-Countries would be bound to make transfer payments to the four other groups in support of climate protection. According to our proposal, the "newly industrialised countries" (NICs) and the "rapidly industrialising developing countries" (RIDCs) will also have to make an active, quantifiable contribution to reducing global emissions in the near future. The NICs could rely on rich nations co-financing some of their measures—and the RIDCs on broad funding of their climate protection by the advanced nations. Without such transfer payments, emission targets for NICs/RIDCs would not become binding. On the other hand, the remaining two groups (ODCs, LDCs) would have to gradually adopt policies and measures for a more climate-friendly direction of their development. Their burden will be to put their full efforts into adapting to climate change.

The key to the indispensable integration of the developing countries into a system of binding emission targets lies in differentiation. For this purpose, the existing country categories will have to be broken up. Even if many of the politicians of the G 77 and China negotiating group still resist the idea, there were already clear indications in Buenos Aires that the unity of the group cannot be maintained without acknowledgement of its members' heterogeneity, The countries most affected by climate change will, for example, no longer tolerate the OPEC countries blocking payments for adaptation measures with compensation demands for possibly declining oil exports.

Several other G 77 countries also gradually recognise the need to move on from the Kyoto Protocol. They are signaling willingness to negotiate. In the medium term, therefore, this group must seek unity in its multiplicity for its own sake and show concern for its own and show concern for the interests of its weaker members. Otherwise the group will lose the negotiating power required to gain necessary concessions from the advanced countries. It goes without saying that the latter have to lead the way in climate protection.

❄ ❄ ❄

Bibliography

Books

Amis, P. (1984), *"Squatters or Tenants, The Commercialisation of Unauthorised Housing in Nairobi"*, in World Development No. 12.

Apodicio A. Laquina (1983), *Basic Housing,* Canada.

Arthur P. Soloman (1975), *Housing the Urban Poor—A Critical Evaluation of Federal Housing Policy,* MIT Press, Cambridge.

Abrams, C. (1964), *"Housing in the Modern World"*, London, Faber and Faber, 24 Russel Square.

Baker, Laurie (1993), *Houses: How to Reduce Building Costs,* Trichur: Centre of Science and Technology for Rural Development, p. 85.

Baldwin, K.D.S. *Problems of Housing in Rural Development,* Norwich: University of East Anglia, School of Development Studies. Vi. p. 57.

Bhargava, Gopal (2001), *Development of India's Urban, Rural and Regional Planning in 21st Century: Policy Perspective.* New Delhi: Gyan Publishing House, p. 309.

Bhaskar Rao, (1989), *Housing and Habitat in Developing Countries,* Newman Group of Publications, New Delhi.

Bayer, Glenn, H. (1959), *"Housing and Personal Values"*, Memoir 364 Ithaca, N.Y. Cornel University, Agricultural Experiment Status.

Bayer, G.H. (1965), *Housing and Society,* New York, Mac Millan Co.

Baskara Rao, B. (1975), *Housing 2000 A.D. —A Long Perspective for India,* Operations Research Group, Baroda.

Borst, F.J. and Jong de.C. (1988), *Slum Improvement in Madras: A Case Study with Special Reference to Cost Recovery,* Amsterdam:

University of Amsterdam, Department of Planning and Demography, Field Work Reports on Housing and Planning in Urban India, No. 6.

Bakshi D. Sinha, (1976), *"Housing Growth in India"*, Arnold Heireman Publishing, New Delhi.

Benerjee, P.C. (1962), *"Industrial Housing by Employers"*, A Relic of Feudalism, I.I.I.R., 1961-1962.

Bhat, Mahesh and Ahamd, V.K. (1970), *Some Aspects of Co-operative Housing Societies in Ahmedabad City—A Case Study,* Gujarat University Publications, Ahmedabad.

Bayer, G.H. & Huge Rose, (1957), *Farm Housing,* A Volume in the Census Monograph Series, New York John Wiley and Sons.

Chester, W. Hartman. (1975), *Housing and Social Policy,* New Jersey, USA, Prentice-Hall Inc.

Clarire Holton Hammod., (1987), *The Benefits of Subsidised Housing Programmes,* Cambridge University Press, USA.

Clark, W.A.C. (1982), *Modelling Housing Market Search,* Croom Helan. London.

Chandhoke, S.K. (1977), *Housing Conditions in Rural India.* I.C.C. Quarterly, Vol. 4, No. 2, pp. 172-183.

Culling Worth, J.B. (1960), *Housing Needs and Planning Policy,* Routledge and Kegan Paul, London.

Culling Worth, J.B. (1966), *Housing and Local Government in England and Wales,* London, Ruskin House.

Chandhoke, S.K. (1990), *Nature and Structure of Rural Habitations,* New Delhi, Concept Publishing,, XXXIV, p.358.

Cherunilam F & O.D. Heggade. (1987), *Housing in India,* Himalaya Publishing House, New Delhi.

Chandrasekhara, C.S., *Integrated Area Development,* New Delhi, Ministry of Works and Housing, p.27.

Chakravarthy B. (1999), *Planning and Management of Rural Housing Schemes in A.P. and Orissa,* Paper Submitted to National Workshop on Rural Housing, NIRD, Hyderabad.

Deutsch, Morton and Marry Evant Collins (1951), *Interracial Housing,—A Psychological Evaluation of Social Experiment,* Minneapolis, University of Minnesota Press.

Dosiadis. A.C. (1976), *The Human Settlements that we Need,* Tata McGraw Hill Publishing Co., Ltd., New Delhi.

Domma Suri, R.P. (1979), *Habitat Asia— Issues and Responses,* Vol.II, Philippines, Concept, Publishing Company, New Delhi.

Dougles H. Keare Scott Parris (1982), *"Evaluation of Shelter Programmes for Urban Poor"*, World Bank Staff Working Papers No. 560.

Dunn, Michael (1981), *Rural Housing: Competition and Choice* by Michael Dunn and Others, New Delhi: Routledge & Kegan Paul, x, p. 277.

Dutt Suresh (1997), *Society and Education,* New Delhi, Anmol Publications, p. 366.

D.R. Veena, Ashok (1985), *"Low Income Rural Housing"*, Ashok Publishing House, New Delhi.

Geofrey K. Payne (1984), *"Low Income Housing in the Third World"*, John Wiley and Sons, New York.

Grebler Leo (1950), *"Production of New Housing"*, Social Science Research Council, New York.

Grims F. Oruille. (1976), *Housing for Low Income Families,* Baltimore, John Aopkins University Press.

Ghanekar, V.V. (1970), *Co-operative Housing,* (Ph.D. Thesis), Poona University.

Grigsby, W.G. (1967), *Housing Markets and Public Policy,* University of Pennsylramia Press, Philadelphia.

Gribsby, W.G. (1967), *Home Finance and Housing Quality in Ageing Neighborhoods,* The Economic Problems of Housing Proceedings of a Conference Held by the International Economic Association Ed. By Adela Alam, Nevitt, Macmillan, London, Melbourne, New York.

Gupta, R.G., *"Planning and Development of Town's"*, Oxford and IBH, New Delhi, 1983, p.237.

Heggade O.D., (1981), *"Financing Housing by Commercial Banks"*, Nagarlok, No. 13(3).

Isler, M.L. (1970), *Thinking About Housing,* Washington, D.C. The Urban Institution.

Jayaram, N. Snadhu, R.S. (1988), *Housing in India—Problems and Prospectives,* D.K.Publishers, New Delhi.

James R. Follain and Emmanuel Zinenez (1983), *"Demand for Housing Characteristics in Developing Countries"*, World Bank Report.

Kelly, Burnham (1959), *"Design and Production of Houses"*, McGraw Hill Book Co., Inc., New York.

Kennedy, R.W. (1953), *The House and the Art of its Design"*. Reinhold Publishing Corporation, New York.

Kalyani, D. (1986), *"Nature of Shelter Improvement in a Slum: A Case Study of M.M. Colony"*, School Planning Ahmedabad.

Keare, D.H. and Parris, S. (1982), *"Evaluation of Shelter Programmes for the Urban Poor"*, Principal Findings, World Bank Staff Working Paper, No. 597. Washington.

Kondapillai, N. (1982), *"Housing the Urban Poor—A Study of Slum Clearance Board Apartments in Madras City"*. Department of Geography, Madras University, Madras.

Laquian, A.A. (1983), *Basic Housing Policies for Urban Sites, Services and Shelter in Developing Countries,* International Development Research Centre. Ottawa.

Leland, S. (1977), Burns and Leo Grebler: *The Housing Nations,* Macmillan Press Ltd., London.

Lennnart J. Lundquist (1986), *Housing Policy and Equality,* Croom Helm Australia.

Madam, G.R. (1976), *Indian Social Problem,* Allied Publishers, Vol. I, New Delhi.

Maisel, Sherman, J. (1953), *House Building in Transition,* Berkeley University of California Press.

Mulk Raj. (1987), *Employment Income and Housing,* Ess Publications, New Delhi.

Michael Dumm, Marilyn Rawson, Alan Rogers. (1981), *Rural Housing Competition and Choice—Urban Regional Studies,* George Allen and Union London.

Ministry of Works (1957), *The Problem of Housing in India,* National Printing Works, New Delhi.

Ministry of Works (1958), *Seminar on Village Housing, Housing and Supply,* Government of India, Missouri.

Muth, K.P. (1969), *Cities and Housing,* The Special Pattern of Urban Residential Land Use, Chicago and London, The University of Chicago Press, Chicago.

Michael Dewit (1989), *Shelter for the Poor in India—Issues in Low Cost Housing,* Manohar Publications, New Delhi.

Mohanthy, A.B. (1988), *Small House: Dimensions of its Planning,* Inter India Publications, New Delhi.

Maclemman, Duncam (1982), *Housing Economics,* Longman Group Ltd., London.

Margaret G. Reid (1962), *Housing and Income,* University of Chicago Press. M. Thaha (1999), Raual Housing in India: PRIs Must Play a Crucial Role, Paper Read at National Workshop on Rural Housing, NIRD, Hyderabad.

Nevitt Adela (1966), *Housing, Taxation and Subsidies—A Study of Housing in the United Kingdom,* London.

Needeman Lionel (1965), *The Economics of Housing,* London Staples Press, London.

Orville F. Grimes Jr. (1976), *Housing for Low Cost Income Urban Families,* World Bank Research Publications, IBRD, Washington, USA.

Parvathamma C. & Satyanarayana. (1982), *Housing in Rural Karnataka, University of Mysore,* Arts Journal, CIo. No. XLIV, March and September, pp. 1-7.

Parvatamma C. & Satyanarayana (1987), *Housing Rural Poor and their Living Conditions,* Gianni Publishers Delhi.

Parvathamma C. (1929), *Housing in Rural India,* Gurunanak Journal of Sociology, Vol.3, No.2, October, pp. 125-144.

Peter J. wan, Emiel A. Wegilin and Komal Panchu. (1983), *Management of Sites and Services Housing Schemes,* The Asian Experience, John Willy and Sons, New York.

Pant N. Balehin. (1935), *Housing Policy: An Introduction,* Croom Helm, Australia.

Poulose Thomas, K. (1988), *Innovative Approaches to Housing the Poor,* Trivendrum.

Ranga Raju, Y. (1976), *Rural Housing in Tamil Nadu,* Sangam Publishers, Madras.

Ramaswami Werma (1979), *Habitat Asia—Issues and Responses on Japan and Singapur,* Vol. III, Concept Publications Company., New Delhi.

Stephen, K. Mayo David, J. (1985), *Sites and Services and Subsidies—The Economic Low Cost Housing in Developing Countries,* World Bank Report, June, No. 83.

United Nations (1957), *Financing of Housing and Community Improvement Programme,* New York.

United Nations (1976), *Guidelines on Housing Policies for Developing Countries,* New York.

Veena, D.R. (1985), *Low Income Rural Housing: A Model for Government Policy and Actions,* Asish Publishers, New Delhi.

Vidya, C. (1987), *Some Aspects of Demand for Housing Finance in Madras,* Operations Research Group, Madras (draft).

V. Suresh (1999), *Budgetary Measures for Housing and Beyond.* Keynote Address Presented at the National Conclave on Housing, Organised by FICCI. New Delhi, p. 11.

V. Suresh (1995), *Basket of Options by HUDCO for Housing Cooperatives,* 11th Souvenir. NCHF, p. 6.

Wood E.E., (1940), *Introduction to Housing: Facts and Principles.* Federal Works Agency, US Housing Authority. Washington DC.

Journals

Arun Kumar, "National Housing Policy: The Implications." *EPW.* June 10, 1989.

Avtar Singh Sahota, (2005), Schemes on Rural Housing, Ministry of Rural Development, *Kurukshetra,* October Room No. 655/661, Nirman Bhavan, A Wing (Gate No. 5), pp. 4-5, New Delhi-110011.

Ananda Yogi (1980), "Novel Features of Rural Housing Schemes", *Yojana,* New Delhi, March 16th.

Balraj Mehta (1988), "Problems of Rural Housing", *Kurukshetra,* New Delhi, November, p. 4.

Chand D. (1986), "Planning for Sound Housing", *Yojana,* 30 (18),

Dastidar S.G. (1983), "Housing Quagmire: A Critical Evaluation of Indian Housing Market", *Yojana,* 27 (5).

Dinesh Chand (1986), "Planning for Sound Housing", *Yojana,* New Delhi, October, p.41.

Francis Cherunilam (1996), "Housing Situation in the Third World", *Southern Economist, Vol.* 25 (17) 33-35,, p. 7.

George K.M. (1989), "Rural Housing Problems and Strategies", *Yojana,* No. 33(3).

Gopal Bhargava & A.K. Jain (1980), "Urban Housing Planning and Policy Implications", *Yojana,* New Delhi, March 16th, p. 27.

George, K.M. (1989), "Challenge and Response of Rural Housing", *Kurukshetra,* Vol. XXXVII, No. 12, New Delhi, September, p. 4.

Habebullah, M.I. (1987), "Housing in the Seventh Plan", Social Welfare, Housing, Vol. XXXIII, No. 11, February, p. 4.

Harichendran, C. (1989), "Housing Development Finance", *Yojana,* New Delhi, July 16-31, Vol. 133, No. 13, p. 21.

Indira Hirway (1987), "Housing for the Rural Poor", *Economic and Political Weekly.* No. 22(34).

Kumar A. (1984), "National Housing Policy—The Implications", *Economic and Political Weekly.* No. 24(23).

Mehta M. & D. Mehta, (1991), "Housing Finance System and Urban Poor", *Economic and Political Weekly,* No. 26(17).

M. Mehta & D. Mehta, "Housing Finance System and Urban Poor", *Economic and Political Weekly,* 26 (17), 1991.

Mathur, G.C. (1989), "Rural Housing Technology and Poverty Eradication", *Kurukshetra,* Vol. XXXVII, No. 12, New Delhi, September, p. 23.

Mahmmod Mamdani, Op. cit., *Economic and Political Weekly* (1976), p. 145.

Navin Chandra Josi (1988), "Critical Issues in Rural Housing", *Kurukshetra,* New Delhi, November, p. 4.

Narayana, N. & Ramanjaneyulu, M. (1990), "Housing Programmes for Rural Poor—A Study in Andhra Pradesh", *Civic Affairs.*

S. Vijaya Kumar & Venkata Ramana, "Rural Housing: An Overview", *Kurukshetra,* 48(10), 2000.

Srinivasan, R.S. (1988), "Appropriate Technologies for Rural Housing", *Kurukshetra,* New Delhi, October, p. 33.

Toy S.S., (1983). "National Housing Policy", *Yojana,* 22(2).

Vijay Kumar S. & Venkata Ramana (2000), "Rural Housing: An Overview", *Kurukshetra,* 48 (10).

Reports

APHSC, *Shelter for the Poor,* Hyderabad, 1990.

A Document on Weaker Sections Housing Programmes in Andhra Pradesh—Managing Director, Hyderabad, 1990.

Andhra Pradesh Economic and Statistical Affairs' Association Arthagananka, Hyderabad, 1985, p. 62.

Census of India 2001, Provisional Population Totals, Government of A.P., Hyderabad.

Census of India 2001, Series-29, Provisional Population Totals, Andhra Pradesh, V. Bhasker. Director of Census Operations A.P.

Council for Advancement of people's Action and Rural Technology, New Delhi, CAPART Guidelines for Dwera Housing IRDP Public Cooperation Rural Sanitation Rural Water Supply Village Link Roads, New Delhi, CAPART, 1996. *Government of A.P., Economic Survey 2002-03,* Planning Department, Hyderabad 2003.

Government of A.P., Statistical Abstract, Directorate of Economics and Statistics, Hyderabad, 2001.

Government of A.P., *Housing Conditions and Migration in A.P., 49th Round,* NSSO, Directorate of Economics and Statistics, Hyderabad, 2000.

Government of A.P., *Report on Housing Conditions in A.P., State Sample 44th NSSO Round,* Directorate of Economics and Statistics, Hyderabad, 1999.

Government of India, *Economic Survey 2002-03, Ministry of Finance and Company Affairs,* New Delhi, 2003.

Government of India, *Economic Survey 2001-02, Ministry of Finance,* New Delhi, 2002.

Government of India, *10th Five Year Plan, Vol. I, Planning Commission,* New Delhi, 2002.

Government of India, *9th Five Year Plan, Vol. II, Planning Commission,* New Delhi, 1999, p. 282.

Government of India, *10th Five Year Plan, Vol. I, Planning Commission*, New Delhi, 2002, p. 19.

General Population Tables, *Census of India, 2001.*

Government of Andhra Pradesh: *Five Year Plans, Department of Finance and Planning*, Hyderabad.

Government of India: *Five Year Plans, Planning Commission*, New Delhi.

Government of India: *Census of India*. 1991-2001, Vol. I, Part-II.

Government of India: *Sociological and Economic Aspects of Housing*, NBO, New Delhi, 2001.

Government of India, the *National Sample Survey, Seventh Round, Preliminary Report on "Housing Conditions"*, No. 26, March 1958, p.1.

Government of A.P., *Housing Conditions and Migration in A.P., 49th Round*, NSSO Directorate of Economics and Statistics, Hyderabad, 2000, p. 2.

Government of India, *Economic Survey 2002-03*, Ministry of Finance and Company Affairs, New Delhi, 2003, p. 217.

Government of India, *10th Five Year Plan*, Vol. I, Op.cit., p. 299.

HDFC, 22nd Annual Report 1998-99, Mumbai, 1999.

HUDCO and Rural Housing—HUDCO, New Delhi, 1981.

Housing Amenities: A Brief Analysis of the Housing Census of India, 1991.

Housing Report and Tables, Census of India, A.P., 1991.

HUDCO, "A Corporate Profile", Presentation to Trainee Officers 1999, HUDCO

ILO, Housing and Employment, Geneva, 1948.

India. Ministry of Agriculture, *Department of Rural Development, Proceedings of the Workshop on Low Cost Housing and Building Technology for the Functionaries of NREP/RLEGP/IAY Scheme in Andhra Pradesh on 6th, 7th and 8th December 1988*, Hyderabad, Regional Housing Development Centre, 1988, p. 81.

India, Ministry of Rural Areas and Employment, *Report of the Sub Group on Rural Housing for IX Plan*, New Delhi: Ministry of Rural Areas and Employment, 1997, p. 28.

India, Ministry of Rural Areas and Employment Indira Awaas Yoiana: Guidelines 1998, New Delhi.

India, Ministry of Works and Housing Western Ghats Region, Tamil Nadu Sub-regional Plan, November 1984.

India, Ministry of Works Housing and Supply, Rural Housing Draft Manual. New Delhi, Publications Division, 1962, p. 72.

India, M/O Rural Development, Rural Housing in India: Problems and Prospects, New Delhi, Rural Housing Section, M/O/R.D., 2000.

Levels of Living in A.P.—Centre for Economic and Social Studies, Hyderabad 1990.

Low Cost Housing for Developing Countries—Central Building Research Institute, Roorkee. 1984.

National Seminar on Housing for the Rural Poor in India—Dept of Structural Engg. Annamalai, University, Madras. 1985.

N.B.O.,—Hand Book of Housing Statistics Part I, N.B.O., Nirman Bhavan, New Delhi, 1996.

Rural Housing at a Glance in India, 1991, As Per Annual Records, Hyderabad.

Statistical Abstract, Andhra Pradesh 2004, Government of A.P., Hyderabad.

Shelter for the Poor in A.P.—The A.P. State Housing Corporation, Hyderabad, 1986.

Shelter for the Poor in A.P. —A.P.S.H.C. A Report of A.P. State Housing Corporation 1989.

Statistical Abstract Andhra Pradesh 2004, Directorate of Economics and Statistics, Government of Andhra Pradesh. Hyderabad.

The Hand Book of Statistics of Adilabad District 2003-04, Compiled and Published by Chief Planning Officer, Adilabad.

Index